THE CHURCH TOMORROW

THE CHURCH
TOMORROW

GEORGE H. TAVARD

HERDER AND HERDER

1965
HERDER AND HERDER NEW YORK
232 Madison Avenue, New York 10016

Nihil obstat: Brendan Lawlor
Censor Deputatus

Imprimatur: Patrick C. Brennan
Vicar General, Diocese of Burlington
October 29, 1964

The nihil obstat and imprimatur are official declarations that a book or pamphlet is free of doctrinal or moral error. No implication is contained therein that those who have granted the nihil obstat and imprimatur agree with the contents, opinions or statements expressed.

262.5
T 197 C

CONTENTS

Foreword   7

1 The End of Sociological Catholicism   9

2 The End of the Counter-reformation   24

3 The Beginning of the Renewal   38

4 Reforming the Church   50

5 Reform of the Religious Life
   through the Liturgy   70

6 The Spirit and the Church   94

7 The Ecclesiology of the Council   115

8 The Ecumenical Dimension   133

9 The Two Faces of Unity   151

10 The Missionary Church   175

Foreword

The renewal of Catholic life which is taking place under the impact of the Second Vatican Council calls for reflection on the implications of such a renovation. The council's decrees, constitutions and declarations will remain dead letter unless they become food for the thought and the life of the members of the Church. It is to be hoped also that they will inspire study and provoke other movements of reform outside the visible limits of the Catholic Church. In any case, this movement of renewal, which started during the Second World War, will continue for a long time and should, in the long run, herald the coming of a new age, not only in the life of the Church, but also in the history of man.

The present volume groups together, around the theme of the reform of the Church, several essays written shortly before, or since, the beginning of the council. Some of them were first cast in the form of lectures, others were published as articles in such reviews as *Jubilee, Continuum, Dialog, Perspectives*. It is my hope that, by reaching a wider audience, they will contribute to the deepening of theological thought without which no renewal can last.

GEORGE H. TAVARD

Mount Mercy College
Pittsburgh, Pennsylvania

1 THE END OF SOCIOLOGICAL CATHOLICISM

There are many different reactions to the Church. One may be equally impressed by her material wealth or by her material poverty, by her high standards of culture or by her lack of culture, by her political detachment or by her political involvement. For the Church as a social body unites extremes. This is indispensable to her universality. Men range from one extreme to its opposite, and to each human perfection or shortcoming there corresponds a facet of the life of the Church in this world.

Among the aspects of her life that are of paramount importance today one should place the balance, in Catholic life, of conviction and of routine. This would deserve to be carefully investigated. To this problem and to its urgency in our day I would like to draw attention. For it may hold a key to much of what is happening to Catholic life, both in Europe and in America.

We may start from a simple, uncontroverted fact: religious convictions create good habits in individuals. Similar habits of many individuals create customs and traditions in the community. Attending Church on Sunday is, first, an act of religious responsibility: Christians who go to Mass do so because they want to share in the Lord's Supper. After a community has acquired the common habit of attending Mass on Sunday, however, this also becomes, besides what it may still mean to individuals, a social gesture. At this point two possibilities lie open. A social gesture may strengthen personal commitment. There will grow a Christian community of which each member is a conscious and free Church-goer. Yet, the social gesture remaining, the religious substance of it may also tend to fade away. In the former case we live in a truly Christian community and, at the national level, in a Christian nation. In the latter case we only have a nominally Christian community and a nominally Christian nation.

The expression "sociological" Christianity, as used here, denotes the stage in the evolution of religion when religious gestures, such as attending Mass on Sunday, have become social habits. Outsiders cannot tell, in this case, whether people follow Mass out of deep-seated convictions or out of social conformity. Worshipers may then be divided into three categories. First, some believe and practice without being dominated by social pressure: they are true believers. Second, some believe and practice largely on account of social pressure, yet they accept the beliefs, unaware that, in so doing, they follow sociological conformity: community and religion have become so united in their mind that they hardly detect the difference between them. The nation tends to identify with the Church; and no true Church member can be opposed to the nation. Third, some maintain the outward practice of religion, although they are inwardly revolted. This revolt may take the form of anticlericalism in politics, of agnosticism in philosophy and of indifference in religion. To these three categories one may add a fourth, made of people who are in open revolt against both Church and society.

The phrase "Catholic nations" and "Protestant nations" are in common use. They apply to countries where Protestantism or Catholicism is dominant and has influenced the social institutions, the philosophical atmosphere and, in a word, the culture and customs of the people. In the so-called Catholic countries, Catholicism is in danger of becoming, or perhaps it already has become, for many persons, a social gesture rather than a living faith. It is a tradition, part of the national heritage, and it is respected as such. In the same countries, there are, or there will be, undercurrents of revolt. For a social gesture becomes meaningless once it is detached from a living faith. It then necessarily breeds guilt feelings, the perennial ground of rebellion.

It may well happen that the minority Catholicism of Protestant or pagan countries is also a "sociological" Catholicism. Catholic practices may be the typical gestures of a group within the nation. They may become, through the years, the characteristic mark of a class, just as antireligion may characterize another class. Religion is often the mark of middle classes, while atheism is that of proletarians. Catholicism may also be the social gesture of a national or racial group in a mixed society, as, for instance, the gesture of the French Canadians in Canada or of the Irish in America. Catholicism is then identified, within the nation, with a minority group. Social pressure within the group may be all the more powerful as the fight for religion and the fight for national survival have been historically associated. The survival of the group has helped it to preserve the faith; and its fight for the faith has helped it to keep its identity. Again one may expect, inside this group, undercurrents of revolt.

When Catholicism has become a social gesture, it is not always moribund as a faith. Faith may lose its purity when social pressure keeps people within the visible bounds of the Church. But movements of liberation from social pressure may aim at deeper spirituality rather than at agnosticism and revolt. Freedom from social pressure may be achieved by rebellion against it, or by ascension above it. The Catholicism of mission territories or of Protestant countries with a scattered Catholic minority is, as a rule, not "sociological"; yet it is not always more dynamic than the "sociological" Catholicism of other lands. Old Catholic countries provide good breeding ground for movements toward deeper spirituality and far-reaching apostolic initiatives. The tradition of a Catholic past is always an excellent starting point for spiritual renovation. A nation that is rapidly turning agnostic may, as a reaction to "sociological" Catholicism, hear a call to new life from the depth of its Catholic tradition. The best trends in its decaying Catholicism may start a surge that will renew the spiritual life of the nominally Catholic mass, and from there it may eventually re-christianize the nation as a whole. Then, presumably, the same cycle will start again. Out of a common faith and a common gesture, religion will again be made into a social requirement. There must follow a loss of substance, a trend to indifference and perhaps a revolt. Many Catholic saints have fanned up fire among the embers of a dying faith; and this had to be done all over again after a few decades.

For a long time now many sections of European society have been alienated from the Church. There are Catholics among them, but social pressure no longer pushes in the direction of Christian belief, morality or practices. In some cases social pressure makes it difficult to behave like a Christian. In Communist countries it tends to outlaw religion. Where it is still alive, religion does not result from blind obedience or blind conformity to a custom.

The case is not so clear in non-Communist countries. Yet it is conventional to say that the Church has "lost" the working class. Actually, however, the working class of European industrial society has not been lost to the Church, simply because, when it was constituted a class during the industrial revolution, it grew outside the areas where Catholicism was a social gesture and a sociological phenomenon—the aristocracy, the bourgeoisie and the peasantry. A fourth class, the industrial workers, was then added to these. It could not be fully integrated into the life of the nation since it did not share the typical religious gesture that united the other three classes. It was out of reach of "sociological" Catholicism. Its struggle with the possessing classes led it to identify religion with the bourgeoisie: the religious gesture became a gesture of alienation, the symbol of its own drudgery.

Meanwhile, another movement took place within the "sociological" Catholicism of the bourgeois classes. Under the impact of the philosophy of the Enlightenment and of the French Revolution, large sections of the bourgeoisie more or less openly revolted against religious gestures. Instead of conforming, they sneered. They sometimes sneered while still conforming. Out of this the "Voltairian" brand of anti-clericalism grew. The gesture of worship, having lost its substance, appeared to be outdated by the gesture of modern philanthropy, which was not based on faith but on reason. Resistance to religious conformity was able to wield wide influence over society. From key positions in politics and in the public school systems of several nations, it undermined "sociological" Catholicism as a whole. Instead of remaining the gregarious action of men who are protected by the anonymity of the conforming crowd, the religious gesture tended to become heroic. A day perhaps would come when religion would require the courage to challenge the universal behavior of a class or a nation. A day would come when Catholicism would no longer be a "sociological" tradition at all.

Has this day now arrived?

Some facts seem to suggest that it has indeed arrived in

some areas. I will take one example. Before the last war most of the vocations to the French clergy came from rural areas. The peasantry was, in fact, except in some more dechristianized regions such as Champagne, Poitou or Saintonge, the last stronghold of "sociological" Catholicism. The middle classes (bourgeois) were still largely Catholic. But those who lived their faith in the middle classes knew that they did so in spite of trends that had been active for a long time in their milieu. On the contrary, a whole village that went to Mass together needed to make no gesture of opposition or even of self-assertion. It only followed a pattern of life that had been set centuries ago in that same village. It used farming methods that had been devised long since. When it modernized its tools, it did so because the new tools could be used with the old wisdom. The Church also was part of the villagers' life and patrimony. Out of the piety that religious customs fostered many vocations grew. At the present time, however, all dioceses and all religious orders in France are undergoing a sharp slump in the number of applicants. A major seminary with which I am well acquainted saw its enrollment go down from one hundred fifty to seventy between 1945 and 1960. This partly corresponds to the low birth rate of the war years (1939–1945). It also comes from the fact that the peasantry no longer provides its former proportion of vocations.

This raises a question: is "sociological" Catholicism losing its traditional hold on the peasantry, as it has already lost it on the bourgeoisie? Since it has never dominated the industrial working class, this would spell, at least in most parts of France, the end of "sociological" Catholicism. Such is, I believe, the case. Through the upheavals of the war, the occupation, the liberation, the anxiety of the post-war time, the instability of the Fourth Republic, the revolution of May 13, 1958, and more recently the Algerian conflict and France's involvement in the Common Market, with the subsequent Paris-Bonn alignment, the French peasantry has been shaken out of its old ways and is not able to find its way back to them. Ancestral customs are being broken by the growing industrialization of farming, by the attraction of cities and by the inroads of tourism. The older restricted village community is giving way. It now lies open to the ways and customs of outsiders. There are instances of this everywhere. "Sociological" Catholicism is breaking down in its last stronghold.

Among the workers' proletariat, Catholicism has been replaced by human hope. Not all workers are Marxist, yet Marxism remains the only philosophy that most of them know. In the middle classes Catholicism still is a vital element even where it has lost its "sociological" hold. This is largely due to the deep-seated individualism of the bourgeoisie: it is not difficult, there, to favor unusual ideas, and therefore it is not heroic to remain Christian even if the major tendency goes toward secularism. The problem is different for the peasantry, which for centuries has been used to collective rather than individual attitudes and motivations. It is too soon to tell if a complete breakdown of religion will take place, or if, in contact with the dynamic Catholicism of Catholic Action movements, the strongest among the rural populations will change their religious ways by ascension. At any rate, what is now taking place may be a most significant development in the history of the contemporary Church in France: the end of "sociological" Catholicism.

Looking at the European situation in general, it is clear that the same factors are at work in other countries. What can be seen in France is also apparent in Germany and in large sections of Italy and Spain. The general weakening of anti-clericalism as a political force may even be a direct consequence of the waning of "sociological" Catholicism. Anti-clericalism has no strength left once the social pressure pushing people to the Church abates. Anti-clericalism seeks, among other things, to defend the liberty of men to be or not to be religious. When social conformity no longer requires a definite religious attitude, the protest of anti-clericals loses its sting. The political success of Christian Democracy in Germany and Italy may well be related to this. The political wisdom of Catholicism may be used once people are no longer forced to accept it under the weight of social pressure. One should not read this as a success for religion or as the spread of a Catholic political domination. It only means that Catholicism is treated on an equal footing with other philosophies. This could not have happened under the regime of "sociological" Catholicism.

The question is: what type of religion will follow the withering of "sociological" Catholicism? This is all the more important as the question is the newer. Never before, in the history of the old Catholic countries, had the problem been brought to the fore. Fortunately, an answer already exists. Not all Catholicism is "sociological." An answer is given, though only a partial one, in the spiritual renewal that has been taking place for some decades now. It is provided in the liturgical movement, in the catechetical revival, in the biblical movement, in the lay apostolate, in Catholic Action. My purpose is not to analyze these, since it has often been done. It is to show the urgency of the situation. The time is not far when we can no longer rely on the influence of the past to keep Catholics in the Church. Family life is no longer patterned on what grandparents would have done. Children will not necessarily follow the way of life of their parents. Schools, in the new mentality, teach a technique, not a philosophy of life. The philosophy of life must be each man's personal discovery.

Such a situation is pregnant with danger. When tradition is no longer the dominant force of a culture, chaos threatens. When principles of thinking and ethics are no longer what schools teach in the first place, a breakdown of intellectual life and of public morality is inescapable. If the conscious behavioral motivations are the outcome neither of deep-seated convictions nor of sociological pressure, they can only result from drives out of the unconscious. One may then explain the prevailing patterns of behavior by reference to instincts of sexual fulfillments or of aggressiveness. The psychology of a man who is no longer actively related to God can only be a psycho-pathology. The collective unconscious of a society where this is predominant can only be a complex of complexes. Society is then ripe for juvenile delinquency on a large scale and for the breakdown of family life, which itself cannot but provoke a disintegration of education.

It is impossible to restore religion directly as a social force when "sociological" Christianity is dying. For one cannot stop the march of a sociological law. One can only restore religion as the ultimate motivation of the personal life. There seems to be only one way of doing this. One must emphasize the elements of personal fulfillment that religion, and especially Christianity, offers. In practice, this means that Catholicism must be presented as the religion of human maturity. The doctrines of sin and redemption justify depth psychology and open a way out of the dilemma of obscure motivations. Man's elevation to the supernatural order through the sacraments redeems him from the yoke of psychological guilt by raising his humanity above itself. The Catholic laity's autonomy in the temporal order must be affirmed, while its participation in the apostolic mission of the Church defines its spiritual maturity. Eucharistic worship, rightly experienced and understood, displays the sovereignty, the "royal priesthood" of Christians. The word of God speaking to man in the Bible reveals an inter-relationship with God in which we are no longer subject to the breakdown of relationships which is rooted in original sin and the consequences of which are explored by modern psychology.

My point of reference so far has been Europe. This is normal. Except for the Moslemized lands of the Near East and of Northern Africa, Catholicism is older in Europe than anywhere else. It is natural that its evolution there, both in good and in bad, should be in advance of the Catholicism of other continents. One may wonder, however, if American Catholicism should be expected to undergo similar stages of decadence and renewal.

We should first determine our point of departure. What is the state of American Catholicism at the present day? This is not a matter of producing statistics about Church attendance, income brackets, conversions or Catholic schools. The sort of inquiry into the effectiveness of the Church that was made, for instance, by the American Institute of Management in 1956 is utterly irrelevant. For whatever conclusions may be drawn from such data, key questions remain unanswered. Thus, is Sunday Mass attendance by American Catholics due to sociological pressure or to personally acquired and preserved convictions? Is the Catholic minority in the United States living in the framework of "sociological" Catholicism? A final answer to these questions should be delayed until the sociology of religious practice in American parishes is more advanced than it now is. We can only attempt to outline a preliminary answer, which we should be ready to revise should contrary evidence turn up.

The recent and unfinished controversy about American Catholic intellectuals seems to highlight two points. In the first place, American Catholicism in general lives in the hothouse of "sociological" religion; in the second, a growing number of Catholics escape this social pressure by "ascension."

Those who have pointed out the lack of intellectual awareness among Catholics have started from a set of values which correspond precisely to what I have called the awakened Catholicism of Europe. They have significantly bemoaned the fact that Catholics like to lie hidden in the intellectual shell of their classroom Thomism and to avoid venturing out on the highways and by-ways of modern scholarship. We have not sufficiently tackled the intellectual problems that our non-Catholic contemporaries are, successfully or not, trying to handle. In order to do this, Catholics of an intellectual bent should, like all true scholars, fight and struggle for knowledge. They must experience in their lives the anguish of searching and the joy of finding. In other words, they must be intellectually adult. An adult is not a man who knows because he has been told: he knows by experience. He has tried to square his faith and the intellectual world of today; and he has found that many modern intellectual endeavors constitute steppingstones toward a new understanding of the relevancy of faith.

Objectors have pointed out that American Catholics have attained a high standard of scholarship. They have cited statistics about college attendance, graduations, membership in the professions. But the question was not whether Catholics are intelligent or educated or successful in professions that imply a good level of knowledge. It was only whether Catholics have acquired, through their years in high school or university, the never satisfied thirst for knowledge which is the mark and the doom of intellectuals. The question concerned an existential quest for knowledge, that is, ultimately, for God as the light of the intellect; and the objection relied on sociological categories, thus showing that it had misunderstood the question.

Should we now wonder why the question was not adequately grasped, the answer is obvious. "Sociological" Catholicism has accustomed us to a peculiar way of looking at Catholic life. We have grown used to placing Catholic things beyond question. Knowing, of course, that individuals are full of shortcomings, we have nevertheless felt that Catholics in general are not: for if they were, the Church herself would bear the blame for it. "Sociological" Catholicism, through a self-defensive reaction, has made us confuse the realm of God's infallible action in his Church and that of man's imperfect response. If the achievements of Catholics in intellectual fields are second-rate, the blame falls on those of them who have enjoyed abilities and opportunities, and yet have misused the first and missed the second. It fastens neither on the Church as a whole nor on the hierarchy. Here again, the reactions of many have been influenced by a fear of divisiveness, which itself arises from a subtle and largely unconscious sociological pressure. Yet the fact that the question of Catholic intellectuals has been raised at all shows that American Catholicism, in some aspects of its life, is now struggling to free itself from inbred sociological pressure in order to become spiritually adult.

The new Catholic life that is called for when "sociological" Catholicism wanes is only a restoration of perennial Catholic elements that "sociological" Catholicism drives into the background: personal responsibility instead of social conformity, lay leadership wherever clerical leadership can be dispensed with, self-education through the liturgical and biblical sources of Catholic piety, psychical maturity through sacramental forgiveness and growth. These are precisely the trends of the awakened Catholicism of Europe. In America it roughly corresponds to what is unfortunately and sometimes uncharitably labeled "liberal" Catholicism.

2 The End of the Counter-reformation

The full meaning of the Second Vatican Council may not appear for several years. Yet it is possible, during the pontificate of Paul VI, to discern some main lines of development for the Church of the future. It is not necessary to be a prophet in order to do this; it is enough to look at the past history of the Church, to know the present needs of the world, and to be acquainted with the opinions and desires that many bishops have formulated in public concerning the council.

If we consider the history of the Church, the trend of our times seems clear. The Council of Trent marked the beginning of the Counter-reformation when the Church took a good look at herself and tried to rebuild some of the things that were partially destroyed toward the end of the middle ages and which had provoked the Protestant Reformation. In this perspective, the council may mark the end of the Counter-reformation, the end of that period of approximately five centuries during which the Church has had to brace herself in order to stand on her own feet after the schisms and divisions of Europe in the sixteenth century. Under our own eyes a certain period is coming to the end. There have been signs in the last thirty years that this is happening. If we read these signs well the council will mark the end of a period and the beginning of a new age.

From the theological point of view, that is, concerning the way we understand dogma and intellectualize doctrine, the council may mark a passage to a new theological spirit. The theological spirit in which we were all raised was the spirit of the Counter-reformation. The Counter-reformation was great insofar as it assisted the Church, strengthening her resources after the chaos of the sixteenth century. Yet, in other ways, it was not excellent. Even the great theologians of the Counter-reformation had to think out their doctrine in reference to the Protestantism they were arguing against; and when one defines his doctrine in opposition to another, he is not likely to have a well-balanced thought. If one is always thinking of the possible objections to his explanation, his explanation will be centered not on the truth he is presenting but on the objections. The result has been a very militant theology with sharp divisions and an easily recognizable structure; but it has given theology the appearance of a fortress, replete with artillery, which is not, needless to say, the best way to understand the Gospel.

We may have wondered at times why John XXIII chose his name. Recent popes chose Pius, Benedict, Leo. Why John? Possibly because the Church where he was baptized was called St. John. But this is perhaps not the deepest

reason. The many Johns who were popes, from John I to
John XXII (and even the first John XXIII), were medieval
popes. In a very interesting and unusual speech about his
predecessor John XXII, John XXIII said many good things
about this man who has been criticized by historians. John
XXIII was simply trying to renew a theological tradition
older than the Counter-reformation. The meaning of his
name is that he was trying to renovate the medieval tradition, or at least some aspects of it; and, beyond the medieval
tradition, he was looking back to the patristic tradition and
to the spirit of the Johannine Gospel.

In June 1962, John XXIII spoke of the "humble Pope of
today, who, not indeed without some apprehension, yet by
a fast decision, chose the name of John, *nomen dulce,
nomen suave, nomen solemne,* as if to remind Christians
and to show that we must love unceasingly, love all the
world, love in all circumstances . . ." On June 20, speaking
to the Central Preparatory Commission of the council, the
Pope made this more explicit: "At the beginning of our
pontificate we decided to choose the name of John, which
had remained in deep oblivion for more than six centuries
(1316–1958). We wanted to bear this name, which is very
dear to us and to all the Church, because it designates two
men who were very near to the Lord Jesus, Redeemer of
mankind and founder of the Church. John, the forerunner,
let us say it again, witnesses to the true light . . . To St.
John, the disciple whom Jesus loved, it was left to transmit
to all ages the great confidences made by Jesus to the
apostles in an intimate conversation . . ."

These confidences of Jesus are placed by the Gospel of John between the last Supper and the death of Christ. This is precisely the place, and therefore the meaning, of the Church: "Between the institution of the holy Eucharist and the sacrifice of the cross, at this place where the evangelical account reaches its climax, the Church, humble and sublime, reflects as it were the features of her divine founder; she reproduces them; and she assumes the very heavy task of bringing light to the nations, of leading men to eternal salvation, of sanctifying human society."

This passage shows the Pope's desire to renew with Johannine tradition, which in the past was especially carried on in the writings of the fathers and the middle ages.

What kind of theology was then developed?

We are familiar with the scholastic theology of St. Thomas Aquinas and of the great Franciscans St. Bonaventure and Duns Scotus, which was renovated in the modern Church under the impulse of Leo XIII. There was also another kind of theology in the middle ages, a theology being rediscovered today, called *monastic*. One theology was built up in the schools and universities; the other in the monasteries and monastic schools. Monastic theology may be called a theology of contemplation rather than of demonstration. Its purpose was not to argue, but to contemplate the mystery of faith under the guidance of the Holy Spirit with the resources of our intellect. Of course, the scholastics themselves aimed at a contemplation of the faith. St. Thomas was a great contemplative, but the way he elaborated his thought was argumentative. He recognized this himself, as we may see from the opinion he ventured, toward the end of his life, that in comparison with the contemplation of God, the *Summa Theologica* was so much straw.

Monastic theology remained near to the theology of the fathers of the Church, who constitute the main source of Catholic tradition. They built their theology through sermons and devotional commentaries on holy Scripture. In other words, their theology, as also the monastic theology of the middle ages, translated their spiritual experience in intellectual terms. Today this is called "kerygmatic" theology: a theology which has as its purpose not the investigation of philosophical parallels, supports and conclusions, but the penetration, the personal existential penetration into the mystery of God that is prerequisite to the proclamation of the word.

There have been many recent discussions on the question: "Is all revelation in Scripture? Or is there a certain amount of revelation which is not found in Scripture but is found in the tradition of the Church?" This may be debated affirmatively and negatively. But such a debate is likely to be representative of the clash of two theologians, of a contemplative theology as distinct from a demonstrative one. Essentially, the position that all revelation can be found in Scripture is not trying to prove anything. It is an explanation rather than a demonstration. To an explanation one may say yes, or no. Yes means that we have obtained some intuition of what the other theologian has seen; no, that God has given us other charisms.

In a recent discussion of this question, the negative position was supported by one main argument: the thesis is interesting, but insufficiently demonstrated.[1] The person who made this point was looking for a theology of demonstration with proofs and arguments. Thus the debate was made at cross-purposes. For the one exponent presented a contemplation of the mystery of the presence of the word in holy Scripture, the mystery of God's speaking to us through the word that he has embodied in the Old and the New Testament; while the other wanted theology to be a didactic sort of demonstration which proceeds by successive systematic arguments toward a conclusion logically acceptable to a philosopher.

I believe that the ecumenical council will mark a departure from the kind of theology which is only a demonstration. Pope John seldom apologized for anything. Admittedly, Pius XII, who was a great Pope in a different manner, often argued points on which Catholics disagree among themselves and with others. He wrote, for instance, on medical ethics, trying therein to justify various tenets of Catholic theology. He spoke on technological society, capitalism and Marxism in attempts to demonstrate Catholic positions. John XXIII adopted a rather different approach, as though he were saying: "This is the Catholic Church. You can take it or leave it. I do not have to argue for it. I do not have to apologize for it."

[1] "Is All Revelation in Scripture?" *Proceedings of the Seventeenth Annual Convention. Catholic Theological Society of America*, 1962, 249–268.

What can the council mean in the field of piety? If all revelation is in some way in holy Scripture, then piety ought to be founded mainly on holy Scripture. This means that many things may have to change little by little; for many of our practices of piety would be difficult to justify from a scriptural angle. We need to return to a more biblical and liturgical worship. On June 2, 1962, John XXIII spoke about piety. There is room for many kinds of pieties, because there are many kinds of temperaments. Not everybody goes to God in the same way, and not everybody is attracted by the Holy Spirit with the same grace. Nevertheless, he added that "always in all things and by all, the sense of Catholicity and universality in faith and in worship must be manifested in the first place." The sense of Catholicity and universality must predominate. Private devotions may be good for some, but they do not express the mind of the Church in her universality and catholicity. The center of Christian piety must always take first precedence; and the forms which piety takes ought to be the traditional forms of the liturgy, rather than the temporary forms of private devotions.

Some time shortly before the council was convened, I was talking with one of the theologians who worked in the preparatory Theological Commission. He spoke of the renovation of piety, wondering how it could be made more liturgical, more centered on the dogmatic elements of faith rather than on somewhat peripheral, eccentric devotions. He suggested that the council was coming too early for this to be realized. Thirty years might be needed to prepare for it. He was hoping that we could develop forms of piety, which too many people feel are new because they are unknown to them, but which are old, because they come from the fathers of the Church and were sanctified by the middle ages. He wished that we could prepare for it for a long time, before the council would come to give it a last push. Then he said: "It will be another religion," using the word "religion" in the Thomistic sense of the virtue of religion by which we are related to God, particularly in prayer. It should be another type of the exercise of the virtue of religion which can take many different forms.

This new type of the practice of the virtue of religion will be more charismatic and prophetic, meaning not that we shall all be great mystics, but that we should be better mystics than we are now. It will be more eschatological, a word which is very popular today among theologians, though unfortunately one which very few else understand. It means that we shall be much more aware of Catholic doctrine concerning the expectation of the second coming of Christ. Christ came once and he created his Church to prepare mankind for his return. The early fathers were very much aware of the expectation of Christ. The Church is here only in expectancy. She has no abiding city here below, and the Christian is not a citizen of this world, but of the world to come. We cannot stop work and merely wait for the second coming of Christ, yet each of us ought to be aware of this expectancy of the Church. The Church has joy here below because she knows that Christ is coming back; and if perhaps we shall not ourselves see his return, he has come back to us through the sacraments. The sacraments are anticipations of the return of Christ. The life of the Church is an anticipation of his return. This will not be just another visit to his friends, but the renovation of the earth and the heavens, the "instoration" of a new earth and a new heaven, as St. John has described it at the end of the Apocalypse. Such a piety will be centered on the word of God who speaks to us today. "I will ask the Father, and he will give you another consoler, to be with you forever, the Spirit of truth" (Jn 14:15–16). Christ still speaks to us. Yet few of us in our piety are really concerned with what he tells us, being anxious about what we tell him.

We should heed John XXIII's injunction in his 1962 letter to the religious orders of women: "Let your prayer be nourished from a profound knowledge of holy Scripture, especially the New Testament, then of the liturgy and the teaching of the Church in all its fullness." The council will promote this type of piety by strengthening the liturgical movement, especially in its general principles of active participation by the layman in the worship of the Church. The layman should not be a stranger praying in the Church while the priest does something at the altar; he must take the place which belongs to him by baptismal right and be as active as the clergy, though in a different manner.

Therefore ought we, for ourselves, and for those for whom we are responsible, to try and develop this type of piety, shying away from individualism and fostering collective worship, as a community experience, as the renewal of the Last Supper when, through a common participation in

the bread and the wine of the Eucharist, the Church came
to be. The Eucharist today is the social event by which the
Church is re-made constantly.

If the council can hasten the transformation of piety
along traditional lines, there are consequences to be drawn
on the concept of the Church. One of the most effective
catalysts in this transformation will no doubt be the Constitution on the Sacred Liturgy. This profound document
states in part (no. 10):

> . . . the liturgy is the summit toward which the activity of
> the Church is directed; at the same time it is the font from
> which all her power flows. For the aim and object of apostolic
> works is that all who are made sons of God by faith and
> baptism should come together to praise God in the midst of
> his Church, to take part in the sacrifice, and to eat the Lord's
> supper.

What, then, we might ask ourselves, is the Church for
us? Some time ago John Tracy Ellis initiated a controversy
by saying that there is a certain amount of anti-clericalism
among American Catholics. And there certainly is some
anti-clericalism, but this anti-clericalism, so-called, is not
bad. It comes from the intuition, which perhaps is not aware
of itself as such, that many of us, particularly in the clergy,
have a working concept of the Church which is neither
quite right, nor quite complete.

We can think of the Church as a power structure, that
is, as an institution in which relationships are defined by

power. This is not false, although, if one says only this, it is far from complete.

Another concept of the Church is possible. John XXIII once spoke of the center of Catholicity, Rome, symbol of the Church, in this significant way:

> The one who is speaking to you has indeed the very high mission of being the Vicar of Jesus Christ on earth and he truly fulfills this mission; but he prefers to call himself *servus servorum Dei*, servant of the Lord's servants. This place where you are is called in the world and in solemn pontifical documents, "Apostolic Palace of the Vatican," a high-sounding name that is fitting on account of the splendors of faith, history and art that are contained in it. But in modern times the custom has grown to call it "the Father's house." Those who live here or who come here from all countries, owe their dignity to the fact that they are, according to the apostles, *domestici Dei*, members of the household of God. They are no longer strangers or guests, but they are established on the foundation of the apostles and prophets, the cornerstone being Jesus Christ.

The lesson is clear: the Church is a fraternity, a fellowship, what is called now a collegiality, a college. We speak of the spiritual college of the apostles, meaning that the apostles were not just twelve men chosen by Christ and having no relation one to the other, each apostle going his own way to preach; rather they were a college because they were unanimous. They agreed on the meaning and the preaching of faith. They worked together. We speak of the college of bishops, meaning thereby not that each bishop is totally independent in his see, but that all bishops together form the teaching Church, expressing the mind of the Church through their unanimity.

The Church then appears as a society in which all the various "orders" of the Church have their say. The place of each of these orders is relative to the others, and none is unimportant. All are necessary. There cannot be a Church without a pope, at least for a long time. Obviously, there cannot be a Church without laymen. The Church in the past was able to be without a pope for several years, but never without laymen. The Church must certainly be conceived as a hierarchy, of which the laity form the first level. But it must be a hierarchy expressing fraternity. This can very well be expressed with a formula contained in the rule of St. Benedict: "Obedience to one another": not only must the layman obey the bishop and the pope, but the pope and the bishop must obey the layman as well. The pope is pope and the bishop is bishop because they are at the service of the Church, including the laymen. They have authority because they have the function of promoting the good of everybody in the Church, including the layman. In this sense, the one in authority must always obey the one over whom he has authority, that is to say, ultimately, the layman.

There is something quite similar in the Exercises of St. Ignatius. The "Rules for Knowing the Mind of the Church" help us to be of one mind with the hierarchy, bishops, priests and laity; they would make us one with the Church, no longer isolated or eccentric, on the outside, but rather one with and in the Church. Elsewhere the Exercises present "Rules to Test the Spirits." The superior has the duty to test the spirits because it is possible for the Holy Spirit to speak through those who are his subjects. Subjects must try to think with the Church, to acquire the sense of the Church, to be in accord with the bishops and the pope. And superiors must test the spirits, in case, when someone has an idea, makes a suggestion or proposes an insight, he would be speaking from the Holy Spirit. It is not only to an audience of housemaids, but to all Christians that John XXIII spoke when he said: "Your activity is a service by children of God to other children of God."

In this sense, the two aspects of the Church—obedience and authority—converge into one. That a certain amount of anti-clericalism is arising is one of the signs that more and more lay Catholics are aware of this dimension of the Church. We should not deny it simply because the word sounds bad. We should understand it. Laymen feel the Church to be a fraternity, "the Father's house," and they are often more sensitive to the values of family life in the Church than are the clergy, who are better prepared perhaps, by training and occupation, to appreciate the relationship of authority. This is an occasion for us to ask ourselves if we think of the Church as a power structure, in which some have power and others do not, or as a fraternity, in which each is united with everyone else and needs everyone else.

Perhaps in five hundred years' time, looking back on the history of our times, historians will say: "The Second Vati-

can Council, which began in 1962, did all these things."
And yet when we read all the acts of the council, a few years
hence, we may have the impression that the council has
done none of them. Perhaps we shall see that all these
points of renovation were more or less adumbrated in the
projects placed before the bishops. I know that all these
points are there. Yet it is possible that several projects will
be shelved. But even if various projects are rejected, there is
no cause for despondence. For the acts of the council will
contain not only what this council has accepted, but also the
various texts proposed to it. This will become a source for
future theologians, and will still inspire the renewal of piety,
of preaching, of teaching. The world, the enlightened laity
and clergy, will have been awakened to the need of reform
and renewal, the renewal that begins and finds its base in
our interior lives and our eucharistic worship.

And even if we cannot at present see such a renewal as the
immediate outcome of the council, it is certain, nonetheless,
that over the years our successors will see it as a result of the
guidance of the Holy Spirit.

3 THE BEGINNING OF THE RENEWAL

John XXIII's announcement that he would call an ecumenical council took the world by surprise. Some people imagined that, the doctrinal infallibility of the Roman pontiff being defined and the administrative work of the Roman congregations being done, on the whole, satisfactorily, there was no need for another ecumenical council. Questions of doctrine could be decided by the bishop of Rome speaking *ex cathedra*, with the safeguards implied in the definition of his infallibility; matters of discipline could be decided by the Roman congregations working in the spirit of his directives.

This is an erroneous assumption. It disregards the fact that the bishops also are doctrinally infallible when they are gathered in an ecumenical council and that the infallibility of the pope was not defined in order to replace that of councils. Together they form two aspects of the infallibility of the Church. It is the Church's infallibility rather than that of the pope which is the ultimate fact underlying all the Catholic tradition.

Another point was also overlooked. The Church as a

society is, like every other society, subject to the historical
and sociological law that brings in a period of decentraliza-
tion after one of centralization. Ever since the time of the
Counter-reformation, the Church has lived under a regime
of centralization; the pontificate of Pius XII brilliantly
continued that tradition. Yet discerning minds have pointed
out for some years that the strength of the Counter-
reformation was spent and that a new age would soon be
opening in the Church's history. It is always imprudent to
venture a prophecy, yet Pope John's pontificate may well
have marked a turning point in the modern history of the
Church and the beginning of a new era.

The task of the council is precisely to inspire the Church
at large with the spiritual impetus necessary to approach
another historical period. The eight councils of the patristic
age—from the Council of Nicea (325) to the Fourth Council of Constantinople (869–870)—were dogmatic councils
which defined the faith in order to protect it from rising
heresies. The seven councils of the middle ages—from the
First Lateran Council (1123) to the Council of Vienna
(1311–1312)—strengthened the Church in its fight for
spiritual freedom from political authority. The three councils of the Renaissance—Florence (1439–1445), Lateran
(1512–1517) and Trent (1545–1563)—were reforming
councils. They changed the ethos of the Church, facilitating
the transition from the middle ages to modern times. The
First Vatican Council (1869–1870), the nineteenth, gave a
final stamp to the work of the Counter-reformation and

helped the Catholic world approach the formidable twentieth century, with its tremendous social, international and scientific upheavals.[1]

What will be the ultimate achievement of the twentieth council? Obviously, it must determine some lines along which a new ethos will develop, the ethos of what Romano Guardini has called "the end of the modern world" or, in the language of Nicholas Berdyaev, "the new middle ages."

We have been living in this new world for some time now. It is natural that, after a certain lapse of time, it should begin to affect the inner life of the Church. It is marked by a number of dominating trends: the growing importance of collectivism at the expense of the rights of the individual; the primacy of the world of labor and technique over the world of leisure and bourgeoisie; the urge to continental or world unity expressed in philosophy, politics and science; the evolutionist attitude, which thinks of man in terms of his unfolding history rather than of his set nature, and of the universe in terms of its extremely long and slow evolution from an indeterminate past to an indeterminate future.

As far as this affects the Church, it means that apostolic methods and forms of piety that were adapted to the men of the last two centuries are becoming less and less adequate.

---

[1] Because of its doctrinal errors on Conciliarism, I do not count the Council of Constance (1414–1418) as ecumenical. In this case the current council is the twentieth, not the twenty-first, as most newspapers have reported it. For an opposite evaluation of Conciliarism, see Hans Küng, *Structures of the Church*, New York 1964.

As someone has said: "You can't preach novenas on Harvard Square." In order to fulfill the traditional function of an ecumenical council, a council today must therefore be primarily a reforming council. It has to establish fully in the new religious mores of Catholics several pioneering movements that have been with us for some time, but have not always been given due recognition.

The liturgical movement comes first, both for its scope and for its maturity. It tries to restore the legitimate place of the layman in the liturgy. We may hope—and I for one am ready to express this as my earnest wish—that the council will not only extend the laity's active participation in the Mass along the lines adopted in the Constitution on the Sacred Liturgy, but will also, in time, give us a vernacular liturgy: the full use of an understandable language would seem to be a reasonable prerequisite of full lay participation.

Another movement of importance is that of Catholic Action as defined by Pius XI: "participation of the laity in the apostolate of the hierarchy." Thus understood, Catholic Action means the development of a spiritually mature Catholic laity. No longer led by the hand like children, laymen must fully assume a responsibility which does not only consist in obeying the clergy, but which entails presenting the Gospel to the secular world. As a result of the council, this adulthood of the Catholic laity should be more widely recognized than it is at present.

The biblical movement too, already well under way in Europe, will deserve attention. It fosters a better knowledge of the Bible by the laity and it develops a Bible-centered piety. This should help the council prepare the end of the individualistic, "devotions"-centered piety which has too often replaced true liturgical and biblical worship.

John XXIII startled Catholics and non-Catholics alike when he singled out the "ecumenical movement" as posing a problem that the council must meet. Many non-Catholics had been under the impression that the Church was not interested in the problem of Christian unity as it faces all Christians today. There is a significant movement toward unity among non-Catholics. The World Council of Churches was set up in 1948 as an agency that promotes and coordinates efforts at Christian reunion. It includes most Protestant denominations, the Anglican communion and several Orthodox churches. Spokesmen for the World Council of Churches have frequently regretted what they consider to be the aloofness of the Catholic Church. They feel that no movement toward unity can be perfectly ecumenical if the oldest and largest Church in Christendom does not participate in it. Until Pope John's announcement, only one official word of encouragement had been given by Rome to the ecumenical movement. That was in an instruction from the Holy Office in 1949, in which the "promotion" of the ecumenical movement was described as being the responsibility of the bishops. Owing to the lack of trained theologians in this field, however, it has been extremely difficult for most bishops to do anything along the lines indicated by the Holy Office. The World Council of Churches has therefore remained confirmed in its impression of official Catholic aloofness, despite the fact that some of its members have enjoyed fruitful private contacts with Catholic theologians. The call by John XXIII, following long years of comparative silence, thus shattered many anti-Roman prejudices, though leaders of non-Catholic churches cannot be expected be greatly impressed by his action until the council's decisions on Christian unity are implemented in the years to come.

In their enthusiasm for the idea of a council, some Catholics—and perhaps some non-Catholics too—have been too sanguine about the possible results of a movement for reunion. In the first place, it should have been obvious from the beginning that Protestant leaders could not have been invited to join in the discussions of the council. An ecumenical council is a gathering of men who stand in the apostolic succession and share the apostolic responsibility of guiding the Church and keeping the deposit of faith. This implies that the immense majority of those attending the council would necessarily be bishops. It was indeed possible to invite bishops whose apostolic succession is traditionally recognized by the Catholic Church even though they are at this time separated from the communion of Rome. Thus the bishops of the Eastern Orthodox Church could have been invited. But it was impossible that the bishops of the Anglican communion could have been in the same position: on historical and doctrinal grounds, their apostolic authority has not been recognized by the Catholic

Church. If the problem of an immediate reunion comes up, it must therefore be restricted to the Orthodox churches, and perhaps to the Old Catholic churches.

Even here, however, we should not be too optimistic. Since the schism between Constantinople and Rome in 1054, there have been two major attempts at reunion. These made by the ecumenical Council of Lyons (1274) and by the ecumenical Council of Florence (1439–1445). Both were outwardly successful and officially ended the schism. And in both cases the schism reoccurred a few years later. These reunions were fated not to last because they were achieved under political pressure rather than on theological grounds, and though union had been officially sealed, the lay people and the lower clergy of Constantinople opposed it.

I shall discuss these ecumenical issues in greater detail later in this book. At present, we can look briefly at two lessons to be learned from these failures. A lasting reunion cannot come from above unless it also expresses the desire of the clergy and laity. I believe that the widespread ignorance about the eastern churches among the Catholic laity would be a major obstacle to ending the schism today. The Orthodox churches cannot accept a reunion with Rome unless they really feel themselves welcome. In other words, the purpose of the council in this matter ought not to be to achieve a reunion with the East there and then, but to determine what obstacles are posed by Catholics themselves to the reunion of the eastern patriarchates, to define what education of Catholics is still needed to make reunion possible, and to take practical steps for such an education.

A second lesson of the past concerns the present political situation. The most important churches of the Orthodox world are the Greek, under the Patriarch of Constantinople, and the Russian in the Soviet Union, under the Patriarch of Moscow. The former could conceivably be tempted to seek reunion in order to be stronger in the face of atheism. This would be renewing the mistakes of the past, when reunion was sought as a means of resisting Islam better; and it is mostly unlikely that such a mistake would be made once more. The Russian church, in turn, would obviously be under such pressure at home, as to impede the serene dialogue without which no such reunion can ever take place. Furthermore, no sections of the Orthodox churches could in conscience reunite with Rome at the cost of breaking communion with some of their sister-churches. There is therefore no chance of the Greeks agreeing to a reunion without the Russians, and vice versa.

The prospects, however, are not hopeless if the aim that we seek is carefully limited. We should fool ourselves were we to believe that only stubbornness on the part of the Orthodox is responsible for the permanence of the existing separation. As regards Christ, the sacraments, tradition, the episcopal office and the infallibility of the Church, the Catholic faith and the Orthodox faith are the same. There are theological differences on the Immaculate Conception, on the Holy Spirit and on the primacy of the bishop of Rome, but these may be reduced by theological explanation.

But there is also, and this is the most significant obstacle, a difference in ethos between the Latin customs that dominate the Catholic Church and the mentality of Greek Christianity that has been preserved by Orthodoxy. The Latin ecclesiastical mind is scholastic and casuistic, while the Orthodox mind follows a more mystical bent. The eastern tradition thinks of the Church as "heaven on earth" and of ethics as *agape* or love, while western theology sees the Church first as an organization and defines ethics in terms of justice. Clearly, there is no contradiction between the two views. But any prospect of a reunion raises many questions. Must the Orthodox Church renounce its ways and adopt Latin theological categories? Must it introduce into its services practices that are foreign to its traditional piety, such as benedictions of the Blessed Sacrament, the rosary, the novenas? Must it pattern its theology on scholasticism and latinize itself by adopting Thomism in its seminaries? To these questions Orthodox tradition must answer in the negative. For us to require or to expect another answer would be to reject a valid part of authentic Catholicism. No reunion can take place at this cost.

This is to say that the council should study how the Greek religious ethos, in which we hear a genuine echo of the Greek fathers of the Church, can find its home in one communion next to the Latin ways of western Christendom without being stifled by them. Once this is done, real progress can be made toward ending the schism of 1054.

The question is entirely different with Anglicanism and

Protestantism. They are separated from the Catholic communion not only by a schism, but also by doctrinal disagreements. It is out of the question to look for practical means of reunion so long as this situation lasts. Churches that deny any of the seven sacraments, as well as the binding authority of doctrinal tradition and the episcopal structure of the Church, cannot expect full unity with the Catholic Church on any terms except through their acceptance of Catholic doctrine. The Anglican communion (or, as it is called in America, the Protestant Episcopal Church) is not purely Protestant. Many of its members are fully Catholic in their beliefs and practices. Yet the Episcopal Church as a whole only permits rather than teaches Catholic doctrine. It cannot therefore be considered, as is the Orthodox Church, a Catholic church.

Yet the ecumenical council can do much toward a future reconciliation with Anglicans and Protestants. It is not enough to call non-Catholics back to the fold and to wait for them to come in one by one. There is room for what the Holy Office has called a "promotion" of ecumenism. This would mean training theologians who can speak to non-Catholics in their own language and can thus unravel misunderstandings that have been piling up since the sixteenth century. The aim of the council in this field should be to encourage the few theologians of ecumenism who are now active, and to take steps to have their number multiplied. If we cannot reasonably expect a reunion in the near future, there is a possibility, at least, that doctrinal discussions may narrow the gap between Catholics and Protestants.

On this assumption, a "Catholic Conference for Ecumenical Questions" has been active in Europe, and several
theological journals in Europe and more recently in the
United States are entirely devoted to ecumenical problems.
Their task is to study and to contribute to the doctrinal
debates that are taking place within the entire Christian
world. Much remains to be done along these lines, but the
council can go a long way toward the full development of
modern ecumenism by encouraging more and broader theological conversations between Catholics, Anglicans and
Protestants.

The task of the council is also to determine what relations
can be developed between Catholic agencies and the many
organizations of the World Council of Churches. The
World Council is not only an organism in which Christians
attempt to reach closer unity, but it is also the inspirer of
many worthwhile and practical initiatives in which all
churches can cooperate without jeopardizing their beliefs.
The absence of Catholics in activities that have no dogmatic
implications (such as charitable endeavors) weakens the
witness of Christian charity in our non-Christian world.
Many practical steps could be taken to reach closer cooperation on this level.

It does not seem that full participation in the World
Council of Churches is desirable for the Catholic Church.
Yet some sort of organic link would be useful to both. For
one thing, it would counterbalance the anti-Catholic voices
that occasionally make themselves heard in the World
Council and thus it would promote peace between Cath-

olics and Protestants. A Catholic representation at the
Geneva headquarters of the World Council could be a
satisfactory way to establish contact without committing
the Catholic Church to the Protestant undertones of much
of the World Council's thinking. It might be noted that
the entry into the World Council of the Orthodox
Churches of Russia, Bulgaria, Rumania and Poland has
effected a profound change. The hope is that Orthodox
pneumatology may help the Council to overcome the difficult problems of unity—and that their entry may in fact
have changed the essentially Protestant aspirations of the
World Council.

These are some of the problems that the ecumenical
council must deal with. I shall reëxamine many of them
more thoroughly as we proceed. Many Orthodox, Anglican
and Protestant Christians in our divided Christendom listen
with respect to the voice of the Catholic Church. Their
attention would be rewarded and their number increased
if the Church took positive steps toward the lessening of
mutual distrust between Catholics and non-Catholics. The
calling of the council and its subsequent study of the question of Christian reunion is by itself a symbolic gesture of
great significance. Pope John and Pope Paul have at least
shown that the Catholic Church does not remain indif-
ferent to the plight of a dismembered Christendom and to
the welfare of the Christians who are separated from her.

4 REFORMING THE CHURCH

From the beginning of the preparation of the council it was evident that, in the mind of John XXIII and of many who worked in the preparatory commissions, the Second Vatican Council was intended to be a council of reform, with a spiritual and pastoral purpose. Being spiritual, it aimed at a more perfect fulfillment of Christ's mission on earth by his disciples the Christians of this century.

With her assistance [the Mother of God] let us continue to exercise our ministry with honor and fruitfulness: our ministry has no other purpose and desire than that the Gospel of Christ be better known by the men of our time, that it be willingly applied and that it enter always more deeply into all the realms of life. Such is the only purpose of the calling of the council . . .

These words were spoken by the Supreme Pontiff to the bishops on December 7, 1962. They linked the idea of the council with the need for a deeper knowledge and a more fervent application of the Gospel. God has manifested himself in the incarnate Lord; and the Church must carry on the task of announcing this good news to the uttermost limits of the earth, so that all men "may have life and have it more abundantly."

This spiritual purpose was essentially pastoral: no man can understand the Gospel in a vacuum. He listens with the intellectual and emotional patrimony into which he was born and educated. The Gospel therefore must be given a new look with each generation. Its eternal truths must be presented anew, not as fundamental innovations, but as traditional substance reaching new men in a new way.

Pope Paul expressed this thought well in his opening discourse at the second session:

> . . . the council is to be a new spring, a reawakening of the mighty spiritual and moral energies which at present lie dormant. The council is evidence of a determination to bring about a rejuvenation both of the interior forces of the Church and of the regulations by which her canonical structure and liturgical forms are governed. . . . Yes, the council aims at renewal.

The purpose of the council implies therefore a renovation of pastoral life and methods. And since pastoral life and methods cannot be severed from the ways and forms of Christian life as a whole, the totality of Christian life has had to come under scrutiny: is it adequate to the task of announcing the Gospel? Or must it be reformed?

The reform of the Church was a familiar concept in the middle ages. Medieval life, as it was experienced then, and as we can follow it through the study of history, was never so holy that it needed no reform. Indeed it was often at a very low spiritual ebb. Time and time again Christians were called to reform themselves. The monastic movements which, to a large extent, constitute the history of the medie-

val Church were movements of reform. The monastic reforms of the Irish monks Columba and Columban in the
sixth and seventh centuries, of Gorze in Lorraine in the
ninth century, of Cluny in the tenth and eleventh centuries,
of Citeaux in the twelfth, were much more than attempts
to reach the ideal monastic life. The monasteries wielded
wide influence over the liturgical and sacramental life of the
Christian society and many bishops were originally monks,
so that monastic reforms usually implied reforms of the
Church. In the thirteenth century the founding of the
mendicant orders, Dominican and Franciscan, were important factors in the reform of the Church which accom-
panied the rise of scholasticism.

Medieval Christians were therefore at home in the idea of
reforming the Catholic Church. Reform had no connotation of heresy, and the great reformers were usually great
saints. When, toward the end of the middle ages, a theological and moral decadence brought about ecclesiastical
chaos, when competing factions of cardinals elected rival
popes to the supreme office, talks of reforming the Church
in capite et membris, "at the head and in the members,"
were current and unabashed. As late as 1537 a commission
of cardinals presented Paul III with a report on the necessity of reforming the Church. And with a sincerity unfortunately misunderstood by Protestants, the Council of
Trent studied and published its decrees super reformatione,
"for reforming the Church."

It should, then, strike us as odd that, since the sixteenth
century, the notion of "reforming the Church" has been

associated with Protestantism, while Catholicism, in the form which it took during the Counter-reformation, seems to have been bent on opposing reform. Counter-reformation did not simply have the connotation of counteracting the Protestant Reformation—that unhappy attempt at reforming the Church which ended in schism and heresy. It also implied, in the minds of many among its supporters, the idea of conserving rather than reforming. Where the Catholic mood in the middle ages had been one of constantly reforming the Church, trying to bring it back to its pristine purity or to bring it ahead to a restored purity, the mood of the Counter-reformation wanted to conserve not only irreformable doctrine, but also provisional, contingent, relative forms of life. The customs and laws of one age tended to be transformed into eternal unchanging ideas. Everyone knows what raising of eyebrows followed the publication in 1950 of Yves Congar's volume: *True and False Reform in the Church*. Even though this book taught perfectly traditional doctrine, its title caused consternation in circles that thought of the Church in the recent terms of conservation rather than in the older, more traditional terms of reform.

Yet the question may be asked: what kind of reform is compatible with Catholic doctrine? Clearly enough, Luther's reformation did not remain faithful to Catholic doctrine. One should therefore define standards of reform before embarking on an experience that could turn into a sad adventure.

The basic ingredient of a Catholic notion of reform will be found in the traditional concept, familiar to the fathers of the Church, of *metanoia*, conversion, penance. We always need to turn ourselves toward Christ, to return to him from our sins, infidelities and weaknesses, to reform ourselves according to his pattern. We always ought to take a better look at his image, to hearken more attentively to his word, to make our interior senses better attuned to the promptings of his Spirit. This conversion figures prominently in the Rule of St. Benedict, where it becomes the center of monastic life. It constitutes the basic motif of the *De Consideratione*, addressed by St. Bernard to Eugene III. It is embodied sacramentally in our sacrament of penance and, I believe, also in the unction of the sick. It is given its share in liturgical worship, beginning with the holy Eucharist, which until recently began in the Latin rite with a penitential psalm (*Judica me, Deus . . .*): "Judge me, O God"; but who would dare to invite God to come as a judge, unless he were willing to do penance?

The things that need to be atoned for are not only our individual sins and secret thoughts. There are also the sins and the mistakes, even if they imply no moral guilt, made in the exercise of public office in the Church. When Gregory XIII in 1572 had a *Te Deum* sung in thanksgiving for the massacre of Protestants in Paris during the night of St. Bartholomew, he committed his office to the injustice of approving a mass murder. Admittedly, he had

been misinformed on the exact nature of the victory that
was reported to him, but misinformation cannot totally
excuse him from a serious lack of judgment. A Protestant
would speak in such a case of the "sins of the Church."
It has become a regular practice, in the assemblies of the
World Council of Churches, to confess the "sins of the
Church" and "of the Churches." The traditional negative
reaction of Catholics to the idea of a "sinful Church" seems
solidly founded on holy Scripture. St. Paul himself, in Eph
5:26ff., speaks of the purity of the Church: ". . . Christ
also loved the Church, and delivered himself up for her,
that he might sanctify her, cleansing her in the bath of
water by means of the word; in order that he might present
to himself the Church in all her glory, not having spot or
wrinkle or any such thing, but that she might be holy and
without blemish." The holiness, which the Creed mentions
as a fundamental mark by which the Church is known
through faith, proceeds from the redemptive holiness of
Christ, who united the Church to himself as his spotless
bride and his mystical body. In keeping with this essential Catholic doctrine, our theology has always shrunk from
any suggestion that the Church as such, although affected
by the sins of her members, would be made by them into
a "sinful Church." The Church conceived as "the congregation of the faithful" is certainly made up of sinners, although it would be more proper to speak of saints who are
not saintly enough. Sinners are made saints by the Church's
holiness, which is a gift of the Spirit and a participation
in the very holiness of Christ. The Church is always holy,

not through the virtues and merits of her members, but through the undeserved, and unrepented, gift of God. Some Protestant ecumenists today certainly wish that the Catholic Church, in or out of the council, would make a confession of sins, and suggest that this would have far-reaching ecumenical results. Some Catholics have been trying, with due caution, to find a way of giving a Catholic sense to the expression "sinful Church." I personally do not think that this line of research can be very fruitful: the phrase "sinful Church" is too ambiguous and it will be better to avoid it. But we should speak of the Church along the traditional lines of thought represented by the concepts of *metanoia*, of conversion, of *conversatio*, of penance, of reform.

If the reform of the Church is seen in the light of this radical return to God, then everything that can be given the aspect of penance, of spiritual purification, of recovery of primitive holiness, may be reformed. In this sense, reform means not giving a new form, but restoring full fidelity to the original form. It implies a reshaping, a restructuring, not that a new structure should be built up, but that the intended structure of the Church should appear more clearly. What has to be shown with all clarity is the original structure. But we must remember that the original structure, because it is God-given, is the abiding framework of the Church's whole life. One cannot think that at some point in the past the structure was lost and may now be discovered again. The Protestant Reformation implied an attempt to find a primitive structure which, the reformers believed, had vanished. This orientation of the Reformation of the sixteenth century could but lead astray from the true underlying structure, which may indeed have become obscured by the theological, liturgical and ecclesiastical decadence of the later middle ages, a decadence which, at least in the case of the liturgy, had started very early in the medieval period. A Catholic notion of reform does not require a search for a lost structure. If there were lost elements of the revelation, a new revelation would logically be needed to find them, so that a search for a primitive Christianity which would have been lost would be just as hopeless as the search for an historical Jesus who would not be the Christ of the Church's permanent faith.

I find it significant of Pope John's concept of the reform of the Church through an ecumenical council that he adopted an unbelievably bold vocabulary in his many addresses concerning the first session of the council. Admittedly, he did not insist much on the notion of "reform" and he spoke little of the "conversion" prerequisite to a restructuring of Church life and institutions. He stressed rather the positive aspect of the same movement: the assistance of the Holy Spirit who inspires the thought, and gives the heart and strength to carry out necessary renovation. The Pope spoke of conversion in equivalent terms. His address to the council fathers at the closing of the first session contained these words: "The council, in its reality, is an act of faith in God, of *obedience* to his laws, of sincere endeavor to correspond with the plan of redemption . . ." It spoke of "the great work of the council" as being "a generous effort to enter completely into God's design." Obedience to God is precisely the virtue which inspires every movement of conversion or reconversion. It is a turning toward God in confidence, fidelity and hope, knowing that he will give us the strength to follow our divine calling.

Obedience or conversion is a receptive attitude to God's gifts. The amazing boldness of John XXIII when he spoke of the renovation of the Church which the council should initiate appears in the striking expression he used: the council will be "a new Pentecost." In the same address we hear these words:

It will then be indeed the new Pentecost, expected with such eagerness, which will enrich the Church with new spiritual powers and will make her maternal spirit and her saving action further to radiate in all realms of human activity. It will be a new forward leap of the kingdom of Christ in the world, a new, ever more profound and persuasive, proclamation of the glad tidings of redemption, the affirmation of the supreme rights of almighty God, of human brotherhood in charity, of the peace promised on earth to men of good will.

After the note of obedience, we now hear the note of a renewal of our understanding of God's designs, that is, a note of *fidelity*. Fidelity implies continuity with the faith of all previous ages, steeping oneself in tradition, continuing the spiritual movements that are implicit in the Catholic structure of the Church and that wait only for the charismatic personalities that will make them flourish.

In Pope John's mind, the time for a charismatic development of the spiritual seeds of the Gospel had arrived. It
had already begun. During the first session, "the one, holy,
catholic and apostolic Church manifested herself to mankind in the splendor of her eternal mission, in the solidity
of her structures, in the persuasive and attractive force of
her institutions." On another occasion, the Pontiff noted
tokens of charismatic effervescence: "It is clear," he said,
"that the grace of the Holy Spirit fills the hearts of the
bishops, of the theologians and of all those who are working
for this imposing assembly."

Another note is patent in the text I have quoted: an
eschatological concern oriented the Pope's thought. The
new Pentecost is not only a continuation of the first, when
the Spirit came down on the apostles, but also an anticipation of the last effusion of the Spirit, when the kingdom
of God will be finally manifested. This world and its
progress are included in God's plan for the coming of the
kingdom of Christ. This may be called an optimism. "Our
century," John XXIII once remarked, "is not so disappoint-
ing as is too often said, all good remaining a privilege of
the past. No, today also and even, may we say, with more
enthusiasm, the heralds of the light are aware of having to
live and to act in order to show the radiance of their Mother
the Church." And the Pope's Christmas message for 1962
pictured the Catholic Church "gathered in council and at
the same time opening herself like the flowering of a new
mankind, reconciled with its Creator, regenerated by Christ
the Savior, in the joy and the peace of souls and peoples."

The Church is the sign of the kingdom of God, which cannot be fully established in this life. The council, where the Church is gathered, is an eschatological event, a pentecostal happening, anticipating the return of all things to God, the final establishment of the kingdom in a new heaven and a new earth.

We have thus obtained three characteristics of a Catholic reform of the Church: obedience to God's high calling, fidelity to the God-given structure, pentecostal opening to the Spirit.

As we noted above, everything in the Church that can bear the aspect of conversion is a proper matter for a reforming movement. The first area that comes to mind is obviously life itself; moral life in the broad sense, that is, the life of a Christian in its spiritual and moral implications. This was the usual scope of reform movements in the past. There is room for infinite improvement in our Christian commitment, in our surrender to God's gracious guidance. No one has reached perfection yet. In a sense even perfection is not a goal to be reached. In his *Life of Moses*, taken as a symbol of the life of a Christian, St. Gregory of Nyssa presents perfection not as a goal to attain, but as a constant marching forward. It is a pilgrimage toward the vision of eternity and the fulfillment of all things in Christ. This is true of the Church, and not only of individual Christians. St. Paul sees the Church as increasing until she reaches the fullness of Christ at the second Advent. Thus, as he writes, "living according to truth and charity, we shall grow in every way toward the one who is the Head, Christ,

from whom the whole body receives concord and adherence
by every joint, when each part works properly, makes bodily
growth and builds itself up in love" (Eph 4:15–16). The
construction of the body of Christ in truth and love is a
task of unending reform, to which each Christian, lay or
cleric, can contribute by reforming himself and his life.

The second area where we can speak of reform without
fear of misgiving is theology. The distinction between faith
and theology, or dogma and speculation, is essential to
Catholic thought, although the private opinions of conservative theologians are commonly mistaken for faithful
translations of infallible truths. Dogma cannot be reformed.
The reason for this is not that dogma is couched in defini-
tions guaranteed by the authority of the Church, although
it is so couched and guaranteed, but that dogma expresses
the word of God despite the imperfection of the human
language it uses; the Church has canonized dogmas because it has appeared at various periods that a certain
formulation of the faith would preserve the reality of the
Christian experience in its totality, while another formulation would be, if not incorrect or false, at least dangerous
for our understanding of Christian realities. To clothe the
invisible in visible words, the ineffable in human phrases,
the eternal in languages that are born, live and die, is the
glory and the inherent limitation of dogma. Because this
is the task of the Church, which is ultimately guided by
the Holy Spirit, dogmatic formulations, once adopted by
the Church, lie beyond reform; the languages used can become dead, the categories borrowed can lose their living

meaning, whereas the substance intended by the Church when the definition was formulated remains ever the same, immutable like the rock on which the Church is built.

Theology has no such status. It is constructed by men who, with all their insights and their technical abilities, are liable to manifold shortcomings. No theological system, even the oldest and the most widely accepted, escapes just criticism. The main criticism that may be leveled at our theology, such as it has been transmitted from school to school since the thirteenth century, is that it has become provincial, our world being now much larger than that of St. Thomas. Scholastic categories are purely western: they represent the mode of thinking of a small geographic section of mankind, leaving the thought of eastern Europe and the Middle East out of account, ignoring central, southern and eastern Asian concepts, being completely out of touch with African ways of thought. Furthermore, they have been frozen in the forms favored by one short moment in the history of western thought, the second half of the middle ages, and not even in all the forms current in that time. Such a provincialism, which is at the origin of a progressively narrow and petrified outlook in theology, risks ending in total sterility. It should be corrected before its deadening effect has paralyzed all areas of thought, making Christians self-centered, fearful and defensive. After seven centuries of repetition, commentary and summing up, our scholastic theology has now reached the limit in irrelevance beyond which it is not safe to venture.

A renovation of theology may follow two principal direc-

tions. It can be renewed by a return to the basic structure of
Catholic thought, through a biblical and a patristic emphasis. Scholasticism was a great theology in its proper
time, because it was, in the culture of that period, biblical
and patristic; it was built through commentaries on the
Bible, which formed the framework of teaching in medieval
schools, and through the study of "sentences," that is,
opinions of the fathers of the Church, as they were known
then. Thanks to more adequate historical methods our
current knowledge of the fathers is more complete than
that of the great scholastics; and our knowledge of the
Bible is more historical and scientific (which does not
mean that it is more complete). On these two counts we
enjoy two excellent points of departure for a renewal of
theology.

Such a renewal must always be made in view of the needs
of our times. The time of the fathers is certainly no more,
and perhaps much less, near to us in terms of culture than
the time of the schoolmen. From this angle there is no
reason to return to the fathers rather than to the middle
ages. It is for our times that we must work, and to the men
of our century that we must present the Gospel. In other
words, the renovation of theology should have a pastoral
direction. Theology must not be an affair of specialists,
made for specialists. Its scope should be the entire people
of God in its spiritual, cultural and apologetic needs today.
Significantly enough, Pope John XXIII insisted from the
beginning that the Second Vatican Council should be essentially pastoral. Yet pastoral activity in the parish level with-

out a solid theological basis would be largely a waste of time ending in agitation without substance. The main task of the council is therefore to orient theology in a pastoral direction. This was made clear in the momentous address pronounced by the Pope on the opening day of the council. The Church, he said, "must ever look to the present, to the new conditions and new forms of life introduced into the modern world, which have opened new avenues to the Catholic apostolate." A pastoral orientation of doctrine requires an appreciative study of modern life and culture in order to see what elements of this modern culture may throw the doors open to the revelation which is Jesus the Lord. What theological forms will develop when Catholics of all continents approach the matter of reflecting about their faith with the treasures of their varied cultural patrimonies, rather than with the scholastic categories inherited from medieval Europe? That is, at this time, anybody's guess. Yet we may hope that new ways of understanding the divine mystery will be pioneered. Aspects of the revelation that medieval culture could not highlight will then, little by little, reach the Church's consciousness, thus carrying the everlasting Catholic tradition a few steps further into the awareness of all truth.

One should not exaggerate the novelty of the idea of reforming the Church. The Catholic Church did not reach the pontificate of John XXIII in a state of total decadence or in immediate need of urgent reform. There have been decadent periods in our past, when the institutional elements of the Church's structure and life seemed to lag behind the spiritual elements. Thus the fourteenth and fifteenth centuries were periods of turmoil, when several popes contended for the succession of St. Peter, when the Hundred Years' War between the French and the English claimants to the throne of France brought unrest to most of western Europe; yet this was also one of the greatest periods in the history of Catholic mysticism, when the Rhenish and English schools flourished, when in France St. Joan of Arc united the most active life to the most profound mystical life. The Church is never in such a sorry state that the interior transformation of souls no longer takes place. Yet it may happen that a gap separates the public life of the institution from the interior life led by the suffering members of the flock of Christ. But our century has not been such a period. It has known no fundamental dichotomy between a reforming movement led by charismatic souls and a continued decadence in the governing spheres of the Church. Far from it: the reforms which Pope John hoped to extend through the ecumenical council started under the previous pontiffs, enjoyed their encouragement, and in some cases proceeded from their initiative.

A few examples will suffice. The liturgical reform, which occupied the largest part in the discussions of the first session, continues the reform of Holy Week by Pius XII and his encyclical *Mediator Dei*, which themselves followed the eucharistic reforms of Pius X. Theological renovation did not wait for the calling of a council, but had been under way for a long time. In our century, it followed the crisis of modernism, and in the last century it was anticipated by such genial theologians as Scheeben and Möhler. The biblical movement, sparked by Lagrange at the beginning of the twentieth century, made headway quietly and effectively, and was endorsed by Pius XII in *Divino afflante Spiritu*. Thus the council did not initiate a reform in the Church; rather it came as a highpoint in a movement of reform which roughly coincides with our century.

Pope Paul expressed the idea of reform well in his opening address to the second session which we quoted above. He continued:

Yes, the council aims at renewal. Note well, however, that in saying and desiring this, we do not imply that the Catholic Church of today can be accused of substantial infidelity to the mind of her divine Founder. Rather it is the deeper realization of her substantial faithfulness that fills her with gratitude and humility and inspires her with the courage to correct those imperfections of human weaknesses. The reform at which the council aims is not, therefore, a turning upside down of the Church's present way of life or a breaking with what is essential and worthy of veneration in her tradition. It is, rather, an honoring of tradition by stripping it of what is unworthy or defective so that it may be rendered firm and fruitful.

A renovation of the Church's pastoral life and methods is therefore expected from the council, if this is indeed to be a council of reform. It would be idle to speculate on what concrete points may have to be changed. For one thing, we cannot expect the council itself, a huge assembly of some 2500 bishops, to work out the practical application of all the decrees and constitutions it will eventually adopt.

This must be left to post-conciliar commissions working along the lines set down by the council. What is needed from us is a readiness to do whatever we can to promote the ends assigned to the council and to adopt willingly whatever concrete changes may be required for the reform that has begun.

Rather than try to obtain a foreknowledge of concrete changes in our ways, and anticipate the image of the Church that will take shape in the decades ahead of us, we ought to form in us the spirit needed to make a reform of the Church vital and lasting. At this time, I can see three points on which we should develop our thought and piety. These are stressed in the first chapter of the Constitution on the Sacred Liturgy.

First, we need a new esteem for the priesthood of the layman, acquired through baptism, which gives us the right and the duty of actively participating in the Church's public worship. In this lies the basis for the liturgical movement, the main goal of which is to increase the laity's participation in worship. As often happens, the theological explanation will reach a new depth from the experience of its priesthood by the laity in the proper order of the liturgy. The doctrine is as old as the First Epistle of St. Peter; but theological reflection about it is lagging, by necessity, as long as the people of God as a whole does not experience the need for it. This need is now coming to the fore, and will be felt more and more as active liturgical participation becomes the norm rather than the exception.

Secondly, we need an awareness of the presence of Christ

not only in his sacraments, but also in the reading of the word. From this we should develop a new sense of the meaning of preaching, the homily forming an integral part of worship and being one of the instruments through which the word penetrates into us, this word of which the Epistle to the Hebrews says: "For the word of God is alive, efficacious and sharper than a two-edged sword, penetrating as far as the point of separation between the soul and the spirit, the articulations and the marrows, judging the feelings and the thoughts of the heart" (Heb 4:11–12).

Thirdly, a new eschatological emphasis in theology and in piety should arise from the work of the council, particularly from its liturgical decrees. The eschatological dimension of worship means that our worship on earth makes us share in that of our High Priest in heaven. We do not take part in our Sunday Masses as in successive exercises strung along the stream of time like beads on a rosary. Rather, through our Sunday liturgy we become present to the death, the resurrection and the ascension of Christ as they are eternally recapitulated in his glorious humanity in heaven. The liturgy implies an anticipation of the return of Christ in glory to judge the living and the dead. Those who take part in it through the exercise of the royal priesthood of their baptism, who have listened to the word and who also channel it in their witness, are already present before the judgment seat of God, where Jesus is "ever alive to intercede for us" (Heb 7:25).

As I have mentioned, these three points are emphasized in the liturgical constitution of the council. In themselves

they have enough spiritual substance to continue and am-
plify the renovation of Catholic life and thought that has
begun. From them there should follow a whole series of
consequences in theology and in the daily living of the
virtue of religion which, in the long run, may "renovate the
face" not only of the Church, but also of the earth. The reform of the Church, which implies our own reform, has
the ultimate purpose of preparing mankind as a whole,
through the acceptance and the overcoming of its modern
dilemmas, to welcome the Savior.

Our function is to save the earth by revealing to it the
face of eternity in a rejuvenated Church.

5 REFORM OF THE RELIGIOUS LIFE
THROUGH THE LITURGY

A superficial acquaintance with the history of the successive reforms of the Church in the past will be enough to show that the successful reforms included a reform of religious orders; and that unsuccessful reforms coincided with a reluctance of religious orders to take upon themselves the burden of reform. A few instances will sufficiently point this out. Medieval reforms of monastic life, such as the reforms of the monasteries of Lorraine in the ninth century, or the Cluniac reform of the tenth century, were starting points of reforming movements of the Church as a whole, which eventually extended their influence throughout the body of Christendom. The Lorraine reform brought St. Leo IX to the see of Rome a century and a half later. The Cluniac movement and the monastic foundations of the eleventh century inspired the reforms that Gregory VII brought to a climax. The Cistercian movement provoked reforms of the Roman See and administration, concerning which St. Bernard wrote *De Consideratione* for the benefit of Eugene III. It is not by accident that the great movement of the friars, in the thirteenth century, led by St. Francis

and St. Dominic, and pursued by their successors, notably
by St. Bonaventure, coincided with the reform of the
Fourth Council of the Lateran and of Pope Innocent III.
Later, the seventeenth century and the great age of the
Counter-reformation, insofar as this implied an interior reform of the Church, coincided with the spread of the
modern religious orders, led by the Society of Jesus and by
the smaller orders which inspired the French School of
spirituality.

A countertest of what may well be a law of the Church's
life may be made. The reforms that did not succeed, during the first half of the sixteenth century, followed an
extraordinary decadence not only of the Church, and
especially of the clergy, as a whole, but also of the religious
orders. Their general unwillingness to reform themselves
may be seen in the rapid disintegration of some of them
in their entirety and of large sections of others in the wake
of the Lutheran movement. If the Council of Trent was
able, though somewhat late, to stem the tide and to orient
the Church toward a serious reform of Catholic life, this
was due, in part, to the belated cooperation of the leaders
of great religious orders, such as Cardinal Seripando, and to
the formation of new orders.

Pope John XXIII once remarked: "History is mistress
of life." That is, we should learn from history in order to
determine our behavior today and tomorrow. It would be
too stupid to repeat the mistakes of the past when they
could be avoided by reflecting on what our ancestors in the
Church did or failed to do. The question is not to point

denouncing fingers at them, but to learn from them as we learn from our parents and from the cultural history of our civilization. If we apply this to the present situation, it is now obvious that the Church has started a vast reform of herself. Many, indeed, when Pope John announced, prepared for and began the council, hesitated to speak of "reform," on account of the supposedly Protestant connotation of the term. Pope Paul VI, however, has openly spoken of necessary reforms not only of the Roman curia, but also of the Church. And there is no valid reason, either in theology, in prudence, or in common sense, to refuse to use the word. The Second Vatican Council is trying to establish theological and canonical bases for a reform of the Church which will enable the Church to face the world of tomorrow, to eschew the dangerous pitfalls that may be discerned, and to recover the position in the world which should be that of the organ of salvation. Will the Church continue to be, what it is in fact today, a dwindling minority well on the way to being insignificant in the civilization of tomorrow? Or will she, on the contrary, recover her place in the new age which is dawning for mankind?

Such a concern must be that of religious orders and not only of the laity at large, who find themselves caught between fidelity to a surviving, if diminutive, Church, and loyalty to mankind at its finest hour when it makes the great discovery of itself as a cosmic unity. There can be no room for religious orders if these appear to be no more than remnants of an outmoded order of things. This should not only concern the bishops and the popes, entrusted with the guidance of the Church as a whole. For the principle of collegiality, of responsibility for all parts of the Christian world and of "solicitude for all the churches" does not only determine the relations of bishops between themselves and with the bishop of Rome; it also determines the relations of all Christians together and the unanimity, in the suffering and militant body of Christ, of all those who have been called to salvation, whether they live in the so-called "world," or in religious houses, or sit in the chairs of authority.

One preliminary objection I shall answer now. One may indeed say that at some moments in the past a serious reform of religious orders was urgently needed for the good of the whole body. Yet one may doubt that such a reform is required today. None of us, I believe, has flagrant examples of contemporary religious decadence in his mind. And it is true, I would think, that religious orders as a whole try sincerely today to be faithful to their vocation, as defined by their founders and as endorsed by the magisterium. This is true; but it is not the question. Reform is not only needed after abuses have taken place in order to set matters straight. Reform is not only remedial. It should also be propedeutic. The question is no longer how to remedy gross abuses and to remove the entrenched privileges of vested interests. It is to contribute to the general revitalization of the Church called by John XXIII and Paul VI, and thereby to prepare the whole Church to fulfill her task in the coming future. The updating of the Church in its theology, in its presentation of the Christian message, in its understanding of the world, in its institutions and administration, necessarily implies an updating of religious orders, in their theology and in the formation of their members, as much as regards theology in general as in relation to the nature and role of the religious life; in their attitude to and participation in the apostolic tasks of the Church, and especially their attitude to the apostolic function of the bishops; in their understanding of the world which, in theory, the members of religious orders have left but to which they are called to return with the message of salvation; in their institutions, in the updating of outmoded customaries, procedures and modes of government. There is no limit to the self-examination that religious orders are called upon to make, if they wish to contribute their utmost to the aggiornamento of the Church.

This theme of "reform" as applied to the religious life I shall consider now from the point of view of the council's Constitution on the Sacred Liturgy. However important is the renewal of a sound liturgical life and however much this should give a new lease of life to all religious orders, the issue is deeper than what commonly goes as "liturgy." The issue lies at the level of worship (if total life is worship) and at that of prayer (if one's whole life is prayer). It is not at the level of the time spent in church as distinguished from the rest of the occupations of religious. Nor is there any necessity here to make careful distinctions between the various kinds of orders, cloistered or not—contemplative or active—orders, regulars or congregations. Before the mo-

mentous issue of the renewal of the Church in preparation
for the nuclear civilization of the twenty-first century, all
orders enter into one category, the category of the old, with
the difference that some are genuinely old while others are
prematurely old. That the old can become new is the
premise from which we start.

I will now draw attention to what seems to me to be the
most significant passage of the constitution in its implications for a reform of the Church in general. The magnificent
description of the liturgy, in no. 2 of the constitution, deserves quoting again and again:

> For the liturgy, through which the work of our redemption
> is accomplished, most of all in the divine sacrifice of the
> Eucharist, is the outstanding means whereby the faithful may
> express in their lives, and manifest to others, the mystery of
> Christ and the real nature of the true Church. It is of the
> essence of the Church that she be both human and divine,
> visible and yet invisibly equipped, eager to act and yet intent
> on contemplation, present in this world and yet not at home
> in it.

The council, in this text, joins two aspects that a canonical approach to Christian life tends to separate, although
traditional theology has always united them, namely *action
and contemplation* (*actione ferventem et contemplationi
vacantem*). It also joins the necessary presence of the
Church in the world through her institutions and the
pilgrim status of Christians, whose citizenship must be in
heaven and who have in this world no abiding city (*in*

mundo praesentem et tamen peregrinam). The Church can never be the one without being the other. Although there is always a human tendency to departmentalize activity from thought, experience shows that without contemplation action is fruitless. There is a tendency to oppose the Church's insertion into the world through her use of the means and methods of modern civilization to own, to prosper, to employ, to distribute and even to sell, and the spiritual poverty of one who owes everything to her divine Bridegroom; yet experience shows that the Church rapidly decays as soon as her interest in worldly efficiency dominates her concern for spiritual poverty. Shall we be efficient and use the means placed at our disposal by society, or shall we pursue our pilgrimage to heaven regardless of our being a scandal to the world? Shall we be actively engaged in converting society, or shall we retire to the desert, there to seek God far from the madding crowd?

The double movement of introspection and prospection is indeed a law of all life. It is normal to find it also in the supernatural life, so that apostolic action must be a fruit of previous contemplation: *contemplata aliis tradere*. The council indeed points out the necessary subordination of one of these poles of Christian life to the other (no. 2):

> . . . and she is all these things in such wise that in her the human is directed and subordinated to the divine, the visible likewise to the invisible, action to contemplation, and this present world to that city yet to come, which we seek.

The human element and the human organization of the Church are sacraments of the divine, which gives them meaning, and which they are destined to manifest. The invisible, known only to faith, attracts the visible, that every man sees, to itself, thus invisibly determining the forms and modes of human action in the Church. Action, which itself proceeds from contemplation, aims at the development of contemplation. It must not be satisfied with forming Christians who avoid mortal sin (whatever mortal sin may be), but it hungers after giving the Lord adorers who will worship him "in spirit and in truth," that is, "in the Spirit and in the Truth," the truth being the Word. To preach the Gospel is not to announce a new fund drive by which people can contribute to the Church and thus manifest their love for the Lord; it is to reveal the mystery of the life of God, Father, Son and Holy Spirit, in which everyman is called to participate by grace. Thus the present realities in the Church should not perpetuate themselves; they should not proliferate, according to Parkinson's law, into endless self-reproductions, which in turn will create their own copies, equally busy and equally useless. The present realities are meant to orient man toward "the future city that we seek." Human life is propedeutic, prophetic of a more permanent life; and the Church's human city is a shadow of the permanent, which is yet to descend from heaven as the New Jerusalem.

We are now at the root of a profound dilemma, which is experienced in all Christian life; we are at the throb of a tension between the present and the future; the temporal and the eternal; the finished, although contingent and liable to destruction, and that which is eternally coming,

eternally growing; the incarnate and the eschatological.
This tension is particularly sensible in the religious life,
which is dedicated to total self-giving, to seeking God by
way of the so-called counsels of perfection, to an explicit
search for holiness. But self-commitment to God in love,
the anguish of seeking and of finding that our search constantly prolongs itself and that the further we go the further
we still have to travel, the experience of God in poverty, in
obedience and in the self-control of complete continence,
are personal and personalizing experiences, so intimate as to
be fundamentally incommunicable, and so structured as to
reach fruition only in liberty. They require spiritual freedom as the very ground on which they can thrive. The
higher one hopes to reach on the way to God, the more
profound must be the root of our actions in Christian
freedom.

The tension of the religious life arises from the fact
that it is led in an institutional framework, according to
rules and constitutions set up in other times for other men
living in other circumstances, and that, however spiritually
sensitive these rules may be to the variety of spiritual temperaments, however respectful they may be of the rights of
the human and Christian conscience, they still cannot cater
to the needs of all and they cannot contribute to the spiritual growth of all without great sensitivity on the part of
those, superiors and confreres, who have to adapt them to
the changing requirements of each person and the moving
circumstances of each day. It is only from a drily canonical
and administrative and, finally, unrealistic standpoint that

problems are resolved by faithfulness to the vow of obedience and by the satisfaction of living within the framework
of a certain set of approved constitutions. The resolution
of spiritual tensions by recourse to canonical categories is,
in final analysis, theologically invalid. It is normal that the
tensions of Christian life—between the human and the
divine, between action and contemplation, between the
visible and the invisible, between the present and the
eschatological—should increase as concern for each of these
bi-polar elements grows. Nowhere should there be more
concern about them than in the profession of seeking after
perfection. The religious life is therefore the place where
these tensions appear in their most naked form. This, as I
see it, is the fundamental problem facing religious superiors:
how can a rule and a law which is made for a community,
for a body of men, be adapted to each? Is each member of
the community expected to adapt himself to the rule, even
at the expense of his own personal, individual vocation, at
the expense of that part of himself which does not belong
to his community, but only to God dwelling in him?

Now it seems to me that the liturgical constitution points
to the direction in which these tensions may be resolved.
Let us continue our reading of no. 2:

> While the liturgy daily builds up those who are within into a
> holy temple of the Lord, into a dwelling place for God in the
> Spirit, to the mature measure of the fullness of Christ, at the
> same time it marvelously strengthens their power to preach

Christ, and thus shows forth the Church to those who are outside as a sign lifted up among the nations, under which the scattered children of God may be gathered together until there is one sheepfold and one shepherd.

The locus where Christian tensions are resolved, where the agonistic aspects of Christian life become integral elements of a higher harmony, is the liturgy. In the mystery of worship, as presented and described here, all the people of God are built up into the holy temple in the Lord. That is, in worship, in prayer as the common experience of the body of Christ in its pilgrim state, each man finds his place in the community. The individual encounters the others in Christ and becomes a person; he experiences community not as a crowd, a collection and conglomeration of individuals or a collectivity where each disappears in a mass, but as a common unity in view of the praise of God in the name of and through all creation. Precisely in common worship does dedication to God lose its too human aspects, its too singular and particular angles, to become assumed in the dedication of the Servant of Yahweh in the name of and for all mankind. Precisely there, what is, at other times during the day, the peculiar occupation and interest of each, becomes the concern of all, because it is assumed in the offering of the Son of Man. Precisely there, each becomes, to the measure of God's grace, the dwelling of God in the Spirit; each reaches to mystical realms of life that are proper to him, yet which belong to all because they contribute, even invisibly, to the adornment of the whole body of the Church. There the religious community, whatever its rule and whatever its way of life, is a cell of the Church and fulfills on a smaller scale what the Catholic Church fulfills on the universal scale. It is the presence of God in the world, ready to enter the world in order to share its sufferings and to announce the good news of salvation. It is the shared presence of the Christ, going to all nations, baptizing them and making them the social body of the Lord. It is the presence of the Spirit, in whom all individualities and all idiosyncrasies acquire a prophetic dimension as they participate in the immeasurable and multi-varied wisdom of God, in the wind which breathes no one knows wherefrom and no one knows whereto.

By being each day reconstructed into the people of the Lord by the liturgy, a religious community becomes a sign for those who are outside. The strength of each member is multiplied so that his preaching the word may be more powerful. Thus the religious community and the religious man become, like the Church, signs raised above the nations, not lording it over them in pride, but illuminating them. "By their fruits you shall know them." By their works you shall know that this is the community of the Lord, where "two or three are gathered in his name." Thus the liturgy affects the entire day, so that what is, at another level, stretched in tension, becomes symbolic of the recovered unity of the children of God.

Once the liturgy has been made the center of religious life, the unavoidable tensions of a community tend to transcend themselves. In worship as the participation of Chris-

tians in the sacrifice of Christ, authority acquires its proper
perspective. It is no longer a canonical prerogative (which
it may legitimately be on another level), but a service. Its
purpose is not the success and the efficiency of a community
and its interior unity in face of the world or in face (as
sometimes happens) of the bishop. The purpose of authority
is the participation of all the members of a community into
preaching the kingdom of God. It has filled its purpose, not
when all have been trained in the practice of unquestioning
obedience, but when the word of God has been announced.
It is meaningful, not when all so-called jobs have been filled
with men, and all men have been assigned their job, but
when ecclesiastical jobs have been replaced by spiritual
responsibilities. Authority deserves to be respected when
it protects the freedom of the children of God. In the liturgical framework, authority is never one-sided, for it is always
mutual. The Lord has authority over the Church indeed,
but only insofar as he gives himself for her and to her. Likewise, a man may exercise authority only insofar as he gives
himself to those over whom he has been placed, that is,
insofar as he obeys them. The paradox of Christian authority is that it is actually obedience: a nonobedient
authority is an abuse. Authority reaches its peak when it
promotes the prophetic qualities of those over whom it
presides. Religious orders in general originated in powerful
prophetic visions which would have been stifled at their
birth if the Church authorities had not, in spite of reasonable misgivings and hesitancies, agreed to let the Spirit
pursue his way in what must have been to them, with their

view of the world, a dark cloud of unknowing. If Innocent III had feared the unknown, the Franciscan movement would have died; but because his authority was an exercise of obedience, the Spirit was not quenched. I shall not pursue the question of finding out how many religious orders, born of a prophetic impulse, have gradually stifled prophetic initiative, in their unavoidable process of institutionalization.

The liturgy is the coming of the kingdom of God, when the Church on earth meets the Church coming down from heaven; when the Christian community, present in this world, learns that she is not of this world; when those who believe in Christ become one body with him, not in metaphor but in truth. Coming out of the liturgical encounter with the divine Presence, the members of a religious community continue to preserve among themselves the relationships that they have experienced in the liturgy. There are no superiors and subjects, but all are one in Christ Jesus. There is "neither Greek nor Jew, neither man nor woman, neither slave nor freeman." There is only a mutual service of each other in the hope that our mutual service will make us better witnesses when we announce the word from the Lord. The one who presides does so by exercising what St. Ignatius of Antioch, speaking of the Church in Rome, called a "presidency in agape." He knows that if he points to his nomination as to the source of his authority, this means very little beyond a neat canonical arrangement. True Christian authority has no visible origin, because it partakes of the authority of Jesus, who replied to those who inquired about the source of authority: "Neither will I tell you by what authority I do these things" (Lk 20:1–8). Christian authority has no visible source because it is the transparency of the Spirit through the Spirit-filled acts of a man, and the transparency of the word through the words of a man. Whoever speaks the word speaks with the authority of the word; and whoever does the deeds of the Spirit acts by the authority of the Spirit.

Such an exercise of authority is essentially creative. For authority, in ultimate analysis, implies a relationship of authorship. On account of what he said and did, the Jews remarked of Jesus that "he spoke like one having authority," and not like the Scribes and the Pharisees, duly appointed and duly educated although these may have been. Of course, there is nothing new in all this. All the great rules point out that a superior, whatever his title, is in reality a servant. But there is always a gap between ideals and facts. The relevance of the liturgical reform at this point is that when the relations of mutual service that exist in liturgical worship are prolonged by similar attitudes in the relationships that bind a community together, abuses of authority and the resulting conscientious conflicts cannot arise.

In this way we come to our first conclusion: the absolute necessity for religious orders to develop a truly liturgical mind. This necessity is absolute, that is, it does not decide what kind of liturgical participation should be developed in the different spiritual traditions of the orders. It does not tend to make Jesuits into Benedictines or Benedictines into

Carthusians. The true spirit of worship should become the core of all communities, whatever their history, their origin, and the apostolic works in which they have specialized.

But if there is no question of changing the "spirit" of any order, there is one of reforming the approach to liturgical practices of most of the orders. The unity of the one altar and one priesthood needs to be recovered in daily life; and we should put an end to the theological and liturgical absurdity of many private Masses every day. The way is now open for a restoration of concelebration; and I see it as an imperious duty of religious orders to promote its practice as much as possible, respecting of course the scruples of those who, out of bad theology, or out of a peculiar devotion, or out of the tyranny of habit, want to celebrate their private Mass everyday.

Another point that needs overhauling is the strange attachment of religious to the most conservative positions possible. I am thinking of the many prayers assigned by some constitutions, directories or customaries which have become more important than the Mass; of the benedictions of the Blessed Sacrament, the novenas and the odd devotions that are so important to many. And most of all I am thinking of all those religious houses that simply drag their feet as regards liturgical reform, persevering in prayers after Mass long after they can be dispensed with, discouraging the people's responses years after the encyclical *Mediator Dei* recommended them, solemnizing a Mass with a Benediction of the Blessed Sacrament at the end, waiting until the very last moment to change what ought to have been changed a long time before, and then introducing the changes in the most confusing way.

At this point we certainly run a danger, which will be the common temptation of diocesan and religious priests: that of replacing an old set of rubrics with a new one. Just as we have had our rubricists, so shall we have them still with us, giving us a revised version of the misunderstanding of the liturgy which sees it as the carrying out of incomprehensible gestures. The words will change, but the tune will be the same. It is the responsibility of religious superiors to see to it that the liturgical spirit is not stifled by rubricism. For this reason the constitution insists on the teaching of liturgy in seminaries and religious houses of study (no. 15), on the major rank to be given liturgical studies (no. 16), on the whole life of a religious house having to be influenced by the spirit of the liturgy (no. 17), on the necessity for priests to lead a fully liturgical life and to share it with the faithful (no. 18). Liturgical life means, in the first place, developing a theology of the liturgy.

I should now develop a connected point, which seems to me to be extremely important today: the liturgical constitution invites us to revise our very conception of the religious life and of its place in the mystical body of Christ. The most remarkable aspect of the text that I am now commenting on is its insistence on the transiency of the visible in the Church, which is but a pointer to the invisible. There is a necessary incarnation of the divine in the human; yet the human is only a way, a passage. One does not stay in a passage. One passes through toward something else, toward a goal which gives meaning and importance to the passage, and short of which one does not stop. That in which one participates is the heavenly liturgy, of which the earthly liturgy is an image and a sacrament. I would like to quote chapter 1, no. 8 on this very point:

In the earthly liturgy we take part in a foretaste of that heavenly liturgy which is celebrated in the holy city of Jerusalem toward which we journey as pilgrims, where Christ is sitting at the right hand of God, the minister of the holy and of the true tabernacle; we sing a hymn to the Lord's glory with all the warriors of the heavenly army; venerating the memory of the saints, we hope for some part and fellowship with them; we eagerly await the Savior, our Lord Jesus Christ, until he, our life, shall appear, and we too will appear with him in glory.

The eschatological emphasis is well marked here. This was to be expected, for the liturgy is an eschatological experience; and a theology of the liturgy will have a strong eschatological flavor. The question which I perceive here concerns the eschatological meaning and status of the religious vocation, which should bring us to the core of our problem, the nature of the religious life. A Church that is deeply aware of eschatological participation in the eternal takes her pilgrim state more seriously than we usually take it. She knows that the kingdom of Christ is not of this world; that she is not a citizen of the earth but that her citizenship is in heaven; that this world, however solid and interesting it appears to be, passes away and only the word of the Lord does not pass away. In these conditions, all our life should be focused on the pilgrim state in which we are, on our passage to heaven, on our orientation toward what eye has not seen and ear has not heard.

In this case, it seems evident to me that there should be no room in our minds for concern about superiority or inferiority, about who is first and who is last in the kingdom of God and in the laws of the Church. The theological emphasis that has been and still is given to the spiritual superiority of the religious state, as a "state of perfection," over the lay state or the simple clerical state, strikes me as entirely out of place. We have conceived the status of the religious in the Church as that of one who makes a profession of seeking perfection. The state of "acquiring perfection" has thus been given not only canonical, but also theological sanction. It is canonically necessary to define the function of the religious, although it would be more advisable not to define it in terms of "privileges" and "exemptions"; but the words that define canonical status need not matter too much, for canon law has never been meant to be taken too seriously. The matter becomes serious when we translate canonical categories into theological speculation. Thus there has developed a theology of the "states of perfection": the people of God is divided in three degrees, that of ordinary Christians, who may seek perfection privately, but do not profess officially to do so; the religious, who by their vows or promises have placed themselves in a state of "acquiring perfection"; and the order of bishops, who, by episcopal consecration, have been placed in a state of "acquired perfection." One knows in what difficulty we run as soon as we try to define the position of the diocesan priest in this scale: the only way to make him fit is either to place him among "ordinary Christians," who are still of and not only in the world, or to give him a share of the "acquired perfection" of the episcopal order. Neither of these solutions makes much sense.

The mistake does not lie in trying to fit diocesan priests into a scheme that has forgotten them. It lies at the basis, in the concept of "state of acquiring perfection" as a theological concept. The notion of "state of acquiring perfection" is unfortunate, in my opinion, for a number of reasons, of which I shall select two:

1. The notion of various "states" within the Church rests on a static idea of orders and hierarchy, in which one can perceive a decadence from the medieval idea of order. The feudal order clearly defined the function of each in Church and society. Function in society was determined basically by birth. Function in Church was determined essentially by participation in a twofold hierarchy: the hierarchy of the sacred orders, to which all, whatever their birth, could accede by receiving the appropriate blessing, ordination or consecration; and the charismatic hierarchy, determined by a more or less complete participation in gifts and charisms given by the Holy Spirit. The former is a hierarchy of function; the latter a hierarchy of holiness. The former is essentially social and visible; the latter essentially hidden, although it may occasionally be perceived through supernatural insight. This is profoundly dynamic, for holiness and perfection are not static but developing

experiences. However, the notion of "state of acquiring perfection" tries to freeze this charismatic hierarchy, the hierarchy of holiness, which essentially transcends all visible limits and escapes ecclesiastical confines, into a set pattern, canonically defined by the three vows.

For the recovery of a dynamic concept of the Church and of functions within the Church, it will be important in the future to tone down, and if possible to do away with, the notion of the religious vocation as somehow superior to the lay vocation, to the married vocation, or to the vocation to the diocesan priesthood. Unless we do this, we shall have the paradoxical phenomenon that while the Church as a whole and her hierarchy are trying to get rid of the "triumphalism" that has developed through the Counterreformation, the religious orders will perpetuate their own "triumphalism" within the Church.

2. A second basic deficiency that I see in the notion of "state of perfection to be acquired" lies in the basis that is sought for it in the New Testament. Unlike the founders of some other religions, Jesus did not found a monastic order and did not organize a religious brotherhood segregated from the surrounding world. Yet we have tried to find a basis, in his words and doings, for making the religious vocation into a somehow superior calling. The distinction between precepts and counsels, which is to be found in so many volumes on the religious life and is heard in so many sermons, is an extremely doubtful one. Certainly the Lord told the young man: "If you wish to be perfect, sell what you own, give it to the poor, and follow me." But between

this text and the theology of the counsels of perfection there is a wide margin. In the Gospel all Christians are called to perfection; and if all are not called to perfection in the same way, this means simply that each has to follow the path of the Spirit for him. There are no two similar ways of perfection. And the so-called counsels are not, in the New Testament, distinct from the precepts.

This is extremely important. For many appeals for religious vocations, based on the distinction between precepts and counsels, take the form of appeals to generosity: if you wish to become perfect, do not stay in the world, where one follows only the precepts of Christ, but go higher, and follow the counsels. This would mean that Jesus defined a way of perfection for some, and a way of imperfection for others. The older and more traditional distinction between the contemplative life and the active life corresponds better to the New Testament and to the implications of the Gospel. But this distinction belongs to the charismatic order, where it may usefully define the ways by which God brings some persons to holiness, but does not help to determine the settled way of life of a community.

The spiritual doctrine of the New Testament is that all are called to perfection and to live according to the precepts and the counsels. But the practice of precepts or counsels has to vary according to the specific function of each Christian in the mystical body of Christ. The difference between religious and others does not lie in the spiritual goals of their lives, but in the specific functions

which they fulfill. And there may be more difference in
the specific functions of two religious of the same order
than there is between religious and laymen in general. In
other words, the religious vocation is much more personal
and much more individual than we have conceived it. It
is not defined simply by joining one particular order; it is
defined by gifts and charisms that each man receives and
that may differ considerably from one to another. It is part
of the function of religious superiors to discern these shades
and nuances in the way the members of the order are
called to walk to perfection, to respect the calls of the
Spirit and the gifts he has graciously given, to mold laws
and regulations to individual vocations rather than to force
individual vocations to fall within a set pattern of laws
and regulations.

What, then, is the meaning of the religious vocation?

I do not think the religious vocation makes theological
sense, except as an epitome, on the smaller scale of the
community or the larger scale of the order, of what the
Church is at the universal level. It is the community of
God with men, which unites men together by joining
them to Christ the Mediator. The religious vocation is a
call to form a liturgical community with others, thus constituting the Church as a local unit. As liturgical, this community not only worships, but also spreads about the word
and the sacraments, the two elements that are fundamentally constitutive of the Church. Some Christians are called

to realize the Church in the community of their marriage. Some are called to make the Church present by devoting their strength, whether they are married or celibate, to transforming the structure of this world and of this society in the image of the divine Life. Some are called to realize the Church, her interior unity in variety, her ecumenical openness and her outgoing missionary zeal, at the level of the diocese under the direct pastorship of the bishop. Others are called to realize the Church as a fraternity of equals devoted to a common purpose according to the specific traditions of a religious order. None of these vocations is superior or inferior to the others. All proceed from the same Spirit.

The specific point of the last one, which is the religious vocation, lies in the special way in which it is prophetic of the kingdom of God: it is a participation in the sharing of all things together in heaven, a sacrament of the communion of saints. Its purpose does not lie in perpetuating itself, but in service. It preaches the kingdom of God by setting an example of total mutual obedience in the fellowship of one common Spirit. It is already on earth the eschatological community, spreading from the center of liturgical action to the periphery of apostolic work.

The nature of the Church is usually studied from the standpoint of the incarnation: the Church is related to him who is, essentially and existentially, her Center, and historically, her Founder, the incarnate Lord. Yet the Lord spoke of the Church not only in terms of himself ("Do this in memory of me"), but also in terms of the Spirit ("He will lead you into all the truth"). In the first case, we do something; in the second, something is done to us. The Church is the realm in which the death and resurrection of Christ has freed the Spirit. The water flowing from the side of the Lord was the Spirit. We find in this expression a condensed formulation of a threefold relationship of the Church: to Christ himself; to the sacramental elements taken from this world but having divine power; to the Spirit who ultimately constitutes the divine power that Christ has brought, who comes out of him, and is unceasingly active, dynamic.

The presence of the Spirit in the Church cannot be an incarnation. Former theologians (Petau, Cardinal Manning) who sought along this line have not been followed.

For if an incarnation is analogous to the origin and the personality of the Son of God ("Born of the Father before all ages, and born of the Virgin Mary in time"), it does not correspond to the origin and the personality of the Spirit. In trinitarian theology, the Spirit is not "born"; He "proceeds" by way of "spiration." Under these mysterious terms, we mean that he is the mutual love of the Father and the Son, the *relational experience* in which the Father experiences the Son as loving, and the Son experiences the Father as loving. The presence of the Spirit must be analogous to this sort of relationship. That is to say: it must be a *relational experience* of love. The Church will be constituted by this experience. It will be the fellowship of those who, in their relations to men, experience the love with which God loves men. There is no need to add that it is the fellowship of those who experience love for God, because, in the words of the Savior, "the second commandment is equal to the first." Such a relational experience is dynamic: it elevates men; in it the Spirit raises us to himself. He who is Fire kindles us, he who is "living breath" breathes life into us, and this life is divine life.

Having noted this as a starting point where we may perceive the link between a theology of the Spirit and a theology of the Church, I shall now proceed to an analysis of some relational experiences that take place in the Church, with the purpose of showing that in them we experience the Church as the living domain of the Spirit of God.

1. THE BEARER OF THE SPIRIT

The Church is the bearer of the Spirit. This is inseparable from the theology of St. Paul on the Church as the "fullness"; of St. John on the "light" or the "life" that is communicated to every believer and makes him one with the Spirit of God; of the Acts, where the Spirit leads the apostles in their task of preaching the Gospel. This can be expressed in terms of collectivity: the Church has received and communicates the Spirit; or in terms of personal experience: the Church is the place where man receives the Spirit and is guided by him.

This carrying of the Spirit is particularly connected with two types of Christian experience.

In the first place, the Spirit is known in an event of which he is also the author: the *event of holiness*. This is an unusual way of speaking. We commonly talk of "reaching holiness," of "becoming holy." Yet holiness is never man's doing. The doctrine of the Council of Orange, that even the beginning of the first step to sanctification is the entire work of God, is a Catholic doctrine. And this is not opposed to the view of the eastern fathers, who tend to see holiness not as a personal quality manifested in the practice of virtue, but rather as a "new world" into which we enter through baptism, a "new being" which we have received, a "new garment" which we have donned. To be holy is not to be virtuous (though it does not exclude it); it is to live in the spirit of paradise before the fall. Redemption precisely takes us back to paradise, into a world which is not a world of sin. The function of the sacraments is just this: to restore us to that world which would be lost if it were not preserved in the human nature of Jesus Christ and to which we are introduced by the Spirit. What we are in ourselves, sinners all, becomes holy in the Spirit when we are translated into the holiness of God. The Church is this recovered world of *innocence*, but *restored* innocence, having gone through the death and resurrection of Christ. Christ is the first Consoler (Paraclete), in that he opens that world to us; the Spirit is the "other Consoler," in that he makes us live in it. In this sense, the Church is essentially the bearer of the Spirit, in which we are transferred by the Spirit into the realm of holiness.

In the second place, the Spirit is not static, but dynamic. He is, in himself, a life, the life of love in God. And love does not stay satisfied with self; it goes out toward the other. In the words of the scholastics, love is "benevolent," it aspires to the good of others; it is self-giving. The page of St. Paul (1 Cor 13) on the qualities of love describes this outgoing propensity, its altruism, its tension. Love is universal in intention; it aspires to a total unity of all, to a communion. Yet love does not tend to a fusion of personalities; it embodies the respect of the creature for her creaturely state. It is realistic and does not long for pantheism. It wants "unity in diversity," or, in a telling expression, it longs for "panentheism," for God-being-all-in-all and for all-being-in-God. If we apply this to the Church as the realm of God's love, it follows that her life will not be static. The Church will not remain satisfied with the boundaries that the first centuries gave her. From its tiny cell of Jewish Christians in Jerusalem, she had to become the Church of the Roman Empire. Then she had to reach the barbarians. Next she had to escape the limits of Europe, and to reach Asia, Africa, America and the Pacific islands. That the *Church is missionary* is not an accident. It is not only the result of enterprising minds. It is the normal consequence of the fact that the Holy Spirit is her guiding spirit. The Spirit of love is universal; it embraces all. It has made the Church the "wave of the future" for mankind, the first fruits of the coming kingdom on the model of paradise. But there is no kingdom of God unless it partakes of the immensity of God. It must have the boundaries of the universe itself. This is why the Church is missionary: she carries the Spirit, and she is carried by the Spirit, to all nations. The unity she reaches is a universal unity, a Catholicity.

The Spirit in the Church thus appears as the motor behind the twofold movement of the Church, toward Catholicity in depth, carrying man into holiness, and toward Catholicity in extension, carrying holiness to all men. Movement implies development. In living beings, it is a growth. For mankind in general, we call it history. The Spirit in the Church makes her life a *history*.

The Church as history is the history of the spiritualization of man. It is the story of the elevation of man by the Spirit of God. It cannot end before man has been totally united to the Spirit of God. The Church as experienced by

Christians implies an anticipation of this total unity. This is anticipated in the sacraments, for they are sacraments of unity, with God, with men and with self. Where there is anticipation, there is also representation. The Church is the *representation of things to come*, because the Spirit makes them already present to her. We thus come to the concept of a *holy typology*.

2.   THE HOLY TYPOLOGY

The Spirit inspires a holy typology. This is only saying that he presides over the life of the Church. As he is himself life, we cannot expect his activity in the Church to be of one type only. In fact, the holy typology is highly diversified, and the Spirit's assistance is equally diverse. According as the final stage of the Church, the reunion of all with all, the total reconciliation on earth and in heaven, is represented by *holy actions*, by *holy writings* or by what we may call *holy ikons*, I would distinguish three elements in this holy typology: the *sacraments*, the *Bible*, the *sacred arts*, corresponding to the sanctification of *matter* (matter used as a divine medium), of *language* (language as an inspired medium), and of the *mind of men* (imagination as a medium of the Spirit). It is a fact that would call for reflection on the ways of God, that the commitment of the Spirit in this holy typology is inversely proportional to the natural spirituality of the medium; it is deepest in the sacraments, and lowest in the arts, the Bible standing in the middle. The sacraments are the works of the Spirit and reach their purpose *ex opere operato*. The Bible, written by the Spirit through inspired writers, is open to misunderstanding, yet conveys, for those who have eyes to see, the sense of the Spirit. The arts—literature, sculpture, iconography—are more remotely related to the Spirit: he is their subject matter, but not their author.

The typology of the sacraments shows that, in the Church, *the filial relationship between the created world and God becomes actual again.* Water is not only water; it is water actuated by the Spirit when it is poured in the name of the Trinity. Wine and bread remain, physically and chemically, wine and bread; but they substantially become the body and blood of the Lord. The relationship of marriage keeps its natural structure; yet it becomes also, for this man and this woman, the actual relationship of Christ and the Church. Penance for sin is no longer man's sole and hopeless work of atonement; it is God's own doing in the death and resurrection of Christ, bringing sinners to new life. Thus the sacraments, in Catholic theology, achieve what they mean, simply because they mean what they are. Doing and being are one. The ultimate reality of the elements is not what they seem, but what they are in the Church. Bread, that nurtures our lives, is intentionally the body of the Lord, members of which we are destined to be. This relationship becomes actual in the Church. The estrangement between matter and spirit is surmounted; they yield to the original sonship that creation meant to be theirs.

In this sense, the Church as typified by the sacraments refers us to the past, namely to the ideal state of creation before sin. But in Hebrew thought the past is also the future. The sacraments have their full scope in the biblical myth of a return to the beginning that will be effective in the future. That is to say, only the final state of the Church will correspond to what mankind was originally meant to be. It will be creation finally restored through the cycle of sin, redemption by Christ and growth in the Spirit. In the anticipation which is effective in the sacraments, this eventual reconciliation of all things with God is made present. The typology of the sacraments represents this. This implies that the sacramental life is not only a *restoration* of paradise and an *anticipation* of heaven, but also a *pilgrimage*. What is given to the unknowing child as paradise, by baptism, will be given as heaven to the adult who has fought the battle of life through repentance (penance, unction), yearning (confirmation), love (marriage) and worship (Eucharist, orders). Thus the sacramental life is the very life of the Church as led by the Spirit from the beginning of the world to its consummation.

Let us now look at the holy *typology of the Bible.* The Bible is historical in that it records a number of historical events relating to the people of God and to the incarna-

tion of the Word. But the Bible is also typological. The
historical events have their meaning not in themselves
taken as bare conjunctions of secondary causes, but in the
center of history, Jesus Christ. God has not only meant to
tell us a story. He has also intended to teach us a lesson.
This is why the Church fathers understood many passages
of the Old Testament as having their relevance in the
Church today. The holy typology here consisted in seeking
for images of things to come, for adumbrations of the fullness of time in what was a period of preparation. And the
Church, in the same spirit, was considered to be itself at
the hinges of two typologies. *In the first place*, she is the
model of which the synagogue was a shadow. The covenant passed between the Father and the Son gave birth
to the Church of the New Testament by replacing the old
covenant between God and Abraham. But the new covenant could replace the old because it had been represented
and anticipated by it. The abolition of the law was its
fulfillment. *In the second place*, the Church herself is not
yet the final stage of development of the purpose of God.
She is the short period between the first and the second
advent, between the fullness of time and the consummation of all things; the eon of the Spirit, in which the Spirit
carries the holy typology one step further. The New Testament is a type of the eternal Gospel that will be promulgated at the last judgment. In the Church herself, then,
there is an *historical reality*, a datum that we have before
our eyes and in which we live; and there is a *spiritual* or
eschatological meaning, another anticipation and re-presen-

tation, referring to the consummation of all things in God.

Thus the holy typology of the Bible shows us the Church to be a history, or rather, to be the history of mankind. There is no history without a purpose and a development. The Church is the purpose of the universe, and her life develops, making the divine purpose progressively more apparent. Admittedly, we should not expect obvious changes from year to year, from generation to generation, or even from century to century. The development in question is in keeping with the dimensions of the universe. We should think in cosmic terms: in light years rather than in solar years. This seems consoling for those who are afraid of the end of the world. But it is a false consolation, for it does not make the end of the world remote for each of us taken individually. Our own death is, for us, the end of the world: it is the end of our world.

I have mentioned a third typology: the *typology of the sacred arts.* I will not develop this point. Yet it would seem as though God had left us a whole field to explore: it is the function of artists to express the desire for God which is at the heart of man. Consciously or unconsciously, they give a voice to creation's aspiration to God. Obviously, this implies an anticipation and representation of the divine in this world, which artists more or less obscurely discern and more or less successfully express. This typology is God-given: it is part of creation. But its clear deciphering cannot be the work of the Spirit such as the typology of the sacra-

ments or that of the Bible. Man's groping for God in the
dark is his privileged experience, in which he reaches to
adulthood. The Spirit is indeed at work here, but he does
not show himself yet, in order that one may seek him
further. Christian artists, however, have created a world
of sacred arts, which partakes of this, yet also partakes of
the typology of the Bible and of the sacraments. Such are
the iconography of the eastern tradition and the liturgical
architecture of the west. The function of this field of research in relation to the Church is to show her as *the fulfillment of man's desire for a communion with the divine.*
In all its monistic or pantheistic, or even agnostic and athe-
istic errors, this desire is expressed in the arts and it reflects
the seed of glory that creation instilled in the heart of man:
the possibility to recognize God if he shows himself and
to be able to say: "We have seen his glory." There is a
Church because there was this possibility first of all. The
typology of the arts implies the divine typology of nature.

Here again the search for the Spirit takes the shape of a
history, of a forward-going movement that never reaches
total fulfillment; and yet at times it anticipates heaven in
an ecstasy of recognition, where art attains to the boundary
of grace.

The threefold world that we have thus investigated is
the Church, inasfar as she is the meeting point of the
creaturely and the divine. She is thus a relation in which
two terms commune. She is the symbol of their communion. She is the instrument also of their unity, which is
used by God to reach man, and is sought after by man who

desires to reach God. This leads us to an attempt to define the Church.

3. THE "ESCHATON"

The Church is the history of the relationship between God and man. This amounts to saying that she is the sacrament of the divine. The typology that we have surveyed shows the Church of the New Testament as the type of the Church in heaven, and the antitype of the Church of the Old Testament. But a type participates in what it signifies. There is no opposition, but participation, between type and antitype. The Church therefore is not only a pilgrimage of man toward God; she is also a growing intimacy of God with man. There takes place in her an ascending and a descending movement, symbolized by the scale of Jacob, up which and down which angels moved. Jerusalem on Mount Sion is a reflection of the heavenly Jerusalem which is already descending from heaven.

This has been expressed in many ways. For Dionysius the Church is a "mystagogy," modeled on the hierarchies of the angels and mediating to man the illuminations of the word. For John Scot Erigena, the Church is a "theophany," the manifestation of God on earth. For Hugh of St. Victor, she is the basic sacramental category, in which sign and reality coinhere. All this is beautifully embodied in the Byzantine liturgy, where the Church appears as already the final kingdom of God. This is marked at the very opening: "Blessed be the kingdom of the Father, the Son and the

Holy Spirit." The chant of the beatitudes prolongs this vision. In the theology of St. Thomas the natural desire to see God provides the link between nature and the supernatural, creation and re-creation: it finds fulfillment only in the revelation, that is, in the Church.

In the controversies of the sixteenth and seventeenth centuries, both Protestants and Catholics tended to lose this vision of the Church as the descending kingdom of God and the fulfillment of the cosmic desire to see him. She was conceived as an "institution" more than as an "event." The invisible reality, perceived only by faith, was overshadowed by the visible institution. The institution was always conceived as the bearer of the Spirit, guided and infallibly protected by him. The stress, however, was not so much on the Spirit as on the channels of his guidance, especially on the bishops and the bishop of Rome. What was underlined was excellent. But excellent elements of the theology of the Church were also slurred over.

Among these was her "eschatological" dimension. When we speak of a holy typology, there necessarily comes a point where all creaturely things (signs) must be referred to their eternal archetype. The fathers spoke of "anagogy," or the representation of eternity in time. The schoolmen spoke of "exemplarism," and they saw the created world as reflecting models or ideas eternally present in the thought of God. All this belongs to the eschatological dimension of the Church. The heavenly Church is identical with the earthly, the invisible with the visible, the eternal with the provisional. The notion of eschatology, however, adds an element to this. It implies that the Church is already experiencing the "eschaton," the last days of the world. The time of the Church is radically evanescent; her center is in front of her, in the final communion of all things, in the reconstruction and renovation of all at the end of this eon. Inasfar as the eternal is present in the Church, the Church has reached the end of this eon. We are waiting for the coming of the Lord in glory, expecting the parousia, the ultimate manifestation of the Spirit who will burn this world and forge a new one in the fire of his love.

I have insisted on the Church as a spiritual history, a growth, a development. I must equally insist that there is no growth unless there is a purpose to it, no development without a climax, no typology without the self-surrender of types, images and shadows, when they meet the Archetype face to face. There is no typology without the hope of such a meeting; and the Christian hope is an absolute certainty. Thus we must say that the Church is not only *the bearer of the Spirit* in this world, *the holy typology* by which the Spirit signifies to us the realities of the life in and with God, or *the history* by which he carries the cosmos to its fulfillment. The Church is also *the* "eschaton," standing in judgment over men and nations.

This calls for a little reflection on the existence of the Church. Time is only the measure of duration. The Church perdures; she exists. This duration is temporal, because it is measured by days, months, years and so on. But it is also spiritual, for the Church lives in the Spirit. St. Bonaventure remarks that the judgments of theologians stand halfway between time (the time of the Church) and oevum (the time of the angels). The same point should be made as regards the Church. She is not angelic, for she is earthly. Yet she is above time through that phase of her existence which takes place in the spirit. Now the Church has not two parts, but two aspects. It is the whole Church which is earthly, and the whole Church which is heavenly. The divine is neither merged into the human (no monophysitism) nor separated from it (no nestorianism); rather, the divine has assumed the human. The earthly visible Church subsists only by the power of the heavenly kingdom of God.

This is to say that the Church is the "eschaton," the last days, not only in hope, but in fact. She not only longs for the coming of the Lord in glory to judge the living and the dead. In her, this very day, the Lord comes to judge the living and the dead. This is what has been called "realized eschatology"; and one may discuss the relative stresses to place on realized eschatology (the eternal here and now), and future eschatology (the eternal at the end of the world). Actually, both are one. A movement is determined by its purpose. The whole life of the Church is eschatological, because it is determined by the eschatology of the last days. But it is eschatological in such a way that already the end is anticipated, the eternal is present. In other words, the duration of the Church takes place in time, but is not subservient to it. On the contrary, it introduces the eternal into this eon. The Church is a new world, in which the substance of the old passes into the new life of the Spirit, "who renovates the face of the earth."

It is not in her own name that the Church passes judgment, but in the name of the Lord. It is through the cross that Christ goes to the resurrection, and through his hiddenness in the hearts of men that the Spirit prepares the glory to come. It is the humility of the handmaid that is exalted. Foolishness to Gentiles and scandal to Jews form the core of the Christian faith. The Spirit has thus effected a *reversal of values*. It must therefore be in her total obedience to the Lord, in her complete surrender to the Spirit, that the Church mediates the eternal. This may be symbolically expressed by the "female" nature of the Church. For St. Paul, she is the bride of the Lord. In the Apocalypse, she is the bride accompanying the Spirit. This alludes to the Jewish theme of the woman-temple, connected with the prophetic comparison of Israel to a woman, faithful, or as the case may be, unfaithful to Yahweh. It is not only the visible Israel, the visible temple, which is feminine. The manifestation of Yahweh is also often feminine: the *Shekinah* (the glory) is female; even the *Rouach* (the Spirit) is a female term. The Christian tradition has used this in the theme of the new Eve, which has been applied to the Church more systematically than to Mary. The Church is the new Eve, the woman crowned with the sun, the mother of the new eon. More recent times have rather shrunk from this vision of the female nature of the Church, and have attributed to Mary many of the feminine attributes that used to be given to the Church. Yet this was no weird mythology. It was just this reversal of values: the feminine virtues of hiddenness, of receptivity, of obedience, of devotion, are precisely the virtues of the Church, much more than the virile virtue of aggressiveness. The ways of the Spirit in this world go through the total surrender of the creature to the Lord. The Spirit does not appear on the market place. His epiphanies happen in the night of faith, in the hidden recesses of the soul. Inasfar as the Church is the channel of the Spirit, she is the bride, redeemed from captivity for her divine wedding, and keeping the attributes of humility even in her glory.

4. THE INSTITUTION

I have now to face a pending question. In this pneumato-logical approach, I have taken it for granted that the Church is both visible and invisible, institution and event. I have tried not to separate both aspects, and I have not spoken of any one of them without linking it to the other. There is not one Church which is the mystical body of Christ, the bride of the Spirit, and another which is the visible institution. In Catholic theology, the visible institution is at the same time the bride of the Spirit. Those ages that had a realistic theology found nothing surprising in this. The realism of the Bible never questioned the fact that a very earthy people, Israel, was the people of God. The early tradition of the Church did not wonder why and how a community of men could be the Church of God.

In the logic of the incarnation, the community of the faithful must be quite as earthly as the incarnate Lord was: they therefore constitute a social body, as he was a human body. The theology of the Spirit is in entire agreement with this, because the Spirit is the Spirit of the incarnate Lord. As he spoke through the prophets of the Old Testament, he next spoke through the apostles of the New. In a different yet connected (analogical) way, he still speaks through the successors of the apostles.

Since a dichotomy was introduced into the western mind this has created a problem. With nominalism first, then with some aspects of Protestantism, and finally with the idealism of nineteenth century philosophy, we find a growing difficulty to conceive of a being which would be material and spiritual at the same time. Now, such is, in the Catholic tradition, the Church: social and mystical, visible and invisible, institutional and the channel of the Spirit. Because Protestants have emphasized the Spirit at the expense of the institution, Catholics have often feared that a focus on the invisible might throw the visible into the shade. This fear is unfounded. For as we have understood the work of the Spirit, the Spirit would not work on this earth unless he had human instruments. He transforms a soul and works through her. He changes a life and this life becomes a channel of his grace. Through the scientific insights of scholars and technicians, he even transforms the cosmos. He makes use of the holy typology, and through it he transforms mankind. Seen from the standpoint of the Spirit, the Church as institution is the necessary instrument of his action. That is to say, the Church must be a social body if the Spirit is to transform society. The institution is destined to act as the instrument of the Spirit. There are, in the institution, several functions: the function of the laity, which is basically a witness, the priestly function of offering the Eucharist, the episcopal and papal functions of teaching. At each level men are channels of grace and instruments of the Spirit. The best rule of behavior would be always to behave in such a way that at this present moment and in this very action we may be the instrument of the Spirit. Then the Church would be a generalized Pentecost. St. Paul was aware of this when he described the Christian life by reference to the gifts and the fruits of the Spirit. Medieval theology, in the same line, saw the gifts of the Spirit as the quickening factors of Christian life. This does not only refer to ethics. It also implies that the charisms which accompany the various functions of the body of the Church are themselves fruits of the Spirit.

It would therefore be fallacious to oppose the institution and the event, the organism of the Church and the breakthrough of the Spirit. The organism subsists through the Spirit and its function is to prepare the breakthrough of the Spirit. This is why St. Ignatius of Loyola formulated two complementary rules: rules to "discern the spirits," and rules to "feel with the Church." The true faith feels with the Church, and the Church is the realm where the Spirit may be perceived. It would be a mistake to deny the Spirit and the freedom of his gifts and inspirations on the ground that we want to have the sense of the Church. But it would also be erroneous to deny the institution because we believe that we have the Spirit. The latter mistake is that of revivalists of all kinds; it necessarily ends in a false mysticism, for the spirit that is opposed to the Church cannot be the Spirit of Christ. The former mistake is that of the Grand Inquisitor who would quench the Spirit because all is given in the institution. The true Catholic mind refuses this choice and the implied contradiction between the Spirit and the institution. He knows that all the glory of the institution is to be at the service of the Spirit.

This makes the concept of tradition all-important: it embodies the conviction that the Spirit has spoken even through noninspired writers. The winding ways of the Church's history have seen a progress of the human mind, led by the Spirit, into the revelation of Christ. Because it is the revelation of Christ, it is given once for all: Christ is ultimate. And because it is only in the Spirit that the Church grasps the revelation, she is led into all truth step by step, as each age becomes providentially able to open its eyes and to see. Just as the men of the past, even through their errors and shortcomings, served the Spirit and were used by him, so will our own errors be employed by the Spirit to enlighten others after us. And if this is true of our failures, how much more so of our true insights? The tradition of the Church's institution is none other than this mysterious but effective action of the Holy Spirit. The institution thus becomes inseparable from the Spirit. Far from being opposed to him, it is the channel of his influence.

Consideration of the Spirit in the Church opens insights into her nature that are not familiar enough to most. Yet the present situation would seem to favor such insights more than the recent past has done. In the Catholic world the Second Vatican Council is seen as a gathering of the bishops under the invisible, yet effective presidency of the Spirit. In the Protestant world there is a growing awareness that new ways must be opened if the deadlock of Christian disunion is to be broken; and who can open new ways but the Spirit? The Spirit "renews the face of the earth" by constantly renewing the Church's lease of life. His presence is assured by the promise of Christ that "I shall guide you into all truth." But he works through men; in a measure, it is up to all of us to contribute to the continuing development of the Church's life.

The movements that are shaking the conscience of Christians all over the *oecumene* testify that the Spirit is still at work.

7 The Ecclesiology of the Council

Let me begin with a short account of a personal experience, which I am sure has been shared by many of those who were and are involved in the inner work of the council. In all the meetings of the Secretariat for Promoting Christian Unity which took place prior to the opening of the council, the members and consultants attempted one thing, namely to think together. We came from many different countries and several continents, with diverse pastoral experiences and theological backgrounds: bishops, professors, writers, preachers, theologians, canonists, all with some standing in connection with ecumenical problems, and several with international reputations. Not all belonged to the same school of thought. We had been trained in many universities, seminaries and scholasticates, in different languages, and we were best acquainted with the German, the French or the Anglo-Saxon traditions of Church life. Few were advanced thinkers, and many could have been described as moderately conservative.

Yet with such a variety of background, experience and even interest, the common effort of thinking together in order to arrive at unanimous positions was made. It was clear from the first that nobody wanted a majority to impose its views on a minority, or even wished to develop in our midst something like "Her Majesty's loyal opposition." The idea was to reach a common mind. Our meetings were not like parliaments where a dominant party dictates its view to the nation, but like the palavers in which I am told the problems of many African tribes are threshed out: open-end debates that continue until unanimity has been reached. Questions where opinions were at the start most diversified came back time and time again, until a common mind appeared. Texts were presented and rewritten any number of times, until they were agreeable to all. And although the number of voting members was small in comparison with the number of consultants, all voices had equal standing during the discussion. On this basis the Secretariat for Promoting Christian Unity worked and prepared a number of schemas for the council.

Such a method of work leads to a discovery: we discover the Church. I do not mean that we found faith in the Church: we had this before; or a doctrine on the Church: we already were able to explain the Church in many ways, from her institutional condition to her meaning as the mystical body of Christ. Those who were interested in history discovered, to some extent, the history of the councils: I learned something about the Council of Trent by taking part in the work of a council and a conciliar commission that I could not have learned by poring over the volumes of diaries and letters of the tridentine fathers; and I think I understand the councils of Ephesus and Chalcedon the better for having shared the tasks of the Second Vatican Council. Yet there is more than this to our common experience of work: we discover the Church not only as a communion of man with Christ, but as a communion of man with man in Christ.

The experience of thinking-together-through a fundamental theological question presents two important dimensions. In the first place, it is thinking together. In our daily experience we think, if we think, alone. We form projects, we devise ways and means to reach our ends and fulfill our purposes. These purposes may be holy in themselves and in their intentions. They may aim at pursuing the good of the Church and saving souls. They may take account of other opinions and views and they may strive to follow accepted behavior among our fellowmen and fellow priests. Yet it remains thinking alone for the Church, while the Church goes by knowing nothing of it, having no part in it, profiting from our thoughts perchance, but having no direct share in their genesis. On the contrary, thinking together presents the dimension of the *Ecclesia*, of the Church as gathering, for "when two or three of you are gathered in my name, there am I, in the midst of them"; of the Church as people of God, in which "people" freely exchange ideas and views in order to arrive at a common mind, which is, precisely, the mind of the Church. Social psychologists and group-dynamic experts tell us of the influence of the group over the thinking of the individuals that are caught in it; they insist on the importance of knowing to what sociological universe we are related in order to assess the real intentionality and meaning of our thoughts and opinions. All of us have experienced the change of climate that occasionally takes place when an unexpected person joins a meeting late: something new happens, which dampens or, as the case may be, excites discussion. But I know of no other case where the experience of being together, talking together, going together slowly toward a common purpose through an agreed expression coincides with the spiritual experience of building the body of Christ, structuring the Church as the gathering of the people of God, communing with Christ through our communing together, formulating what we hope will be the thought of the Church.

The second dimension is that of thinking-through. This is important because it assigns unanimity rather than majority as the goal to be reached. The element of unanimity brings to mind the Acts of the Apostles describing the early Church waiting for the descent of the Holy Spirit at the third hour: "All with one heart were assiduous in prayer, with some women, among whom Mary, the Lord's mother, and his brothers" (1:14). Majority may be reached through power-political combinations, pressure group tactics and more or less underhanded lobbying. Unanimity can be reached only through spiritual maturation. To be unanimous in the Church implies listening to the other as to one through whom the Spirit may be speaking to me now, balancing his words as though they were possibly conveying the word of God now. It implies speaking as though our words could be prophetic, assumed by a Power higher than

ours, and charged with a meaning that we ourselves cannot
fathom. Unanimity means placing ourselves at the disposal
of the Spirit for his Church, for her purification, for the
better manifestation of her holiness, her apostolicity, her
catholicity and her unity. It means including into our
thoughts the criticism that may be formulated and which
it ought to undergo in order to reach maturity. It means
speaking after we have been criticized rather than in order
to forestall criticism, knowing the truth of these words of
Paul VI to the officers of the Roman curia: "It is understandable and providential that such a phenomenon (criticism) should happen now and again in the history of the
Church. It incites watchfulness, it recalls us to observance,
it invites reform, it is a leaven of perfection. We must welcome the critics around us, with humility, with reflection
and even with gratitude." Unanimity is not attained by
way of an Hegelian dialectics: thesis, antithesis, synthesis,
or partly true, partly false, true. It comes to light by discerning together the mind of Christ and the message of
the Spirit for our times. What one man, even the highest
in the Church, cannot do alone, all can do together, when
all place their lights and insights at the disposal of the
Spirit to enlighten the whole body of the Church.

Despite the tedious length of its debates, the cumber-
some number of persons involved, and its outdated procedures, the council has had a similar effect on most of its
participants. It also has been for most an experience of
thinking-together-through some of the religious problems
of our day. This is the sense of a remark heard from a

bishop, that the council was for him what his tertianship
is to a Jesuit. It is also the sense of this statement of a well
known theologian, that the council is a "celebration": it is
not a meeting, a convention or a parliament, but the celebration of the coming down of the Spirit upon the apostles
at Pentecost. This is the sense of the many occasions in
which John XXIII expressed his conviction that the Second Vatican Council would be "a new Pentecost."

These personal experiences are highly relevant, for they
highlight the first ecclesiological lesson of the council. The
ecclesiology of the council does not reside first of all in
whatever texts on the nature of the Church it has debated
and will eventually approve. It resides in the first place in
the implications of the fact of the council. Since October
11, 1962 the Church has been living a conciliar life. The
activities of its members have not remained isolated, but
have been part of a vast movement of self-criticism and
self-reform. The experience of thinking together may be
reserved, in its most vivid form, to a few hundred persons,
yet through them something is surfacing from the depths
of the Church's conscience. The council manifests that the
whole Church is a conciliar experience, that the fraternity
that many have sought—sometimes in vain—in religious
communities and priestly gatherings exists nowhere better
than at the level of the Church as the people of God in
pilgrimage toward heaven, trying to formulate its spiritual
insight. It has revealed that, however much the Church
may look like a power structure, however much authority
may be wielded unjustly and tactlessly, however much it

may be exercised with ignorance and imprudence, the Church at bottom is intended to be the brotherhood in the Holy Spirit of those "who have been called to be saints." Not only in the upper room with the apostles, or at a council now and again, is the mark of the Spirit seen, do the tongues of fire come down, does unanimity in prayer and intention take shape through the sharing of thought and purpose! The Church is destined to be, at all times and in every place, the communion of man with man in God. The tragedy is that few can say with the fervor of St. Teresa of Avila: "I am daughter of the Church." Because she had this basic experience of the Church as communion, St. Joan of Arc could confess, at the very moment when bishops, canonists, and theologians were looking for a pretext to condemn her for heresy and witchcraft: "The Church, I love her, and would like to help her with all my power for our Christian faith."[1] How many would follow her to the extremity of confessing the Church when the churchmen who confronted her cared so little about the basic relationship of unanimity in the Church, when they were so little disposed to listen to a laywoman who, in this case at any rate, was the prophetic instrument of a message from God?

Whether we liked the idea of it in the first place or not, the council is now an historical fact with a meaning for the theology of the Church: it means precisely that at this particular moment, though for all times, the Church is

[1] Quoted by Raymond Oursel in *Les Procès de Jeanne d'Arc*, Paris 1959, 81.

taking a "new look" at herself. What she is discovering
is also what our fashion magazines call a "new look." It is
something very old, as fashions usually are, though it appears now in the trimmings of novelty for the simple reason
that we had forgotten it: the Church is not only the body
of Christ extended throughout the world and throughout
time, or a social institution with her structures, her traditions and her ethos; she is also a communion of man with
man, a brotherhood, a fellowship, a collegiality or, more
simply, a catholicity, all words which convey various aspects
of the same fundamental quality of the Church. They con-
note what St. Paul called *koinonia* and which was variously
entitled by the fathers *concordia*, *agape*, *eirene*, or, with
St. Augustine, *catholica pax*, the dimension of unanimity,
of forming one soul together. This is nothing new. It has
been sung by many generations of Christians: *o quam
bonum et jucundum habitare fratres in unum*; or, *con-
gregavit nos in unum Christi amor*. The liturgy extols *vera
fraternitas*. Holy Scripture constantly refers to the *ecclesia*,
the gathering of those who were dispersed, in which bar-
riers fall down and there is no longer "Jew or Greek, slave
or free man, man or woman, for you are all one in Christ
Jesus" (Gal 3:28). The congregation at Mass is *plebs tua
sancta*, "your holy people," made one in holiness. The
offering is that of *cunctae familiae tuae*. Yet how much of
this has passed, I would not even ask, in the daily life of the
faithful, but only in our personal concepts of the Church?
What does the word "Church" evoke in our mind? Indeed it is likely to raise up the image of a church building

or any other image of power, rather than that of a community in which all things are shared, an image of humility. The inferior status and function of the laity until recently in most areas and still today in many is an obvious sign that our working concept of the Church has not done justice to the biblical and traditional idea of the Church as the community of the people of God.

The practical problem of the council is to translate this insight into authoritative texts that are destined to nourish the Church for decades and centuries, and that may, in a short while, by presiding over the formation of seminarians, change the mind of the clergy for the better. The directives given by the two conciliar popes, John XXIII and Paul VI, are unambiguous. The council and its works must be essentially "pastoral." Pastoral concern was beautifully described as a dimension of all theology by Paul VI in an address of September 6, 1963, a few days before the second session:

It would be imprudent to see the importance given pastoral activity as an oblivion of theological speculation or as something destined to compete with it; theological speculation keeps its dignity and its excellence, even though the imperious necessities of the Church's life require that sacred doctrine does not remain purely speculative, but that it be considered and fostered in the full framework of Christian economy, that is, as a doctrine that has been given us to practice true religion, to be preached to souls and to manifest its saving virtue in historical reality. Today, intellect and will, thought and labor, truth and action, doctrine and apostolate, faith and love, magisterium and ministry have, in the Church's life, complementary functions, that are always closer and more organic, for their splendid mutual development.

This truly magnificent text clearly points the way to a pastoral activity governed by theological contemplation, and to a pursuit of theological reflection entirely oriented toward its practical fulfillment in the life of the whole people of God. The still prevalent dichotomy between research and application, between theology and care of souls, between liturgical prayer and services for the people, between seminary or college and parish, between chair and pulpit, must give way to a deep conviction of their complementary functions and of their mutual responsibilities. The question is not so much of finding ways to dovetail these concerns and activities. It is in the first place to realize the meaning of such a fecundation of action by contemplation and of thought by experience.

The Constitution on the Sacred Liturgy, which was promulgated by Paul VI on December 4, 1963, embodies this integral approach to the mystery of the Church:

The liturgy by which, especially in the divine sacrifice of the Eucharist, that task of our redemption is done, supremely provides that the faithful express and show others by their life the mystery of Christ and the genuine nature of the Church, which is both human and divine, visible yet with invisible qualities, fervent in action and devoted to contemplation, present in the world and nevertheless on pilgrimage. In this way, the human in her is oriented toward the divine and subordinated to it, the visible toward the invisible, action toward contemplation, her presence toward the future city that we seek. Thus, while the liturgy daily builds up those who are in the Church into a holy temple in the Lord, a dwelling of God in the Spirit, until the measure of the fullness of Christ is reached, in a wonderful way it also strengthens them to preach Christ, and thus it shows the Church to those who are outside as a sign raised above the nations, under which the dispersed children of God are gathered into one until there be but one flock and one shepherd.

The theological plenitude of this text rivals its pastoral implications and concerns. Or rather they are one: it is theology in the total unfolding of its pastoral dimension.

The ultimate test of the council, however, relates to the decree on the Church, where the integral approach to action and contemplation should be at its best. In it the experience of catholicity as Catholic unity which implies oneness in plurality should be fully manifested. The unity of those who are and remain diverse is not only a horizontal unity of men of "every nation, race, people and tongue" (Ap 7:9), among whom "there is neither Greek nor Jew, neither slave nor freeman, neither man nor woman" (Gal 3:28); it is also the unity of many functions ordered toward one purpose. "There is indeed diversity of spiritual gifts, but the same Spirit: diversity of ministries, but the same Lord; diversity of activities, but the same God who works all in all. To each the manifestation of the Spirit is done for the common good" (1 Cor 12:6–7).

This implies collegiality not only at the highest level of the hierarchy as the collegiality of bishops for the government and guidance of the universal Church. It implies also the collegiality of the whole people of God, laymen, priests and bishops being one under the same Spirit for the service of the same Lord, in the diversity of their callings and charisms. We have too often given the impression of being a Church not only of authority, but also of dictation, the only absolute monarchy left in the world, an outmoded example of spiritual tyranny, intent on its rights and advancements and respecting the liberty of others only insofar as it does not stand in its way. This criticism at any rate has been leveled at the Church from the right and from the left. For this reason it is important that all—and not only the bishops at the council—should try to answer the question formulated by Cardinal Suenens: "Church of Christ, what do you say of yourself?" It is equally important that the answer given to this should not only embody correct doctrine, but should also express it intelligibly for those who throughout the world are asking the question.

I need not go at this point into any details concerning the constitution on the Church which was debated in the first half of the second session of the council and adopted in the third. I will simply make some general remarks that do not apply only to the text itself, but to the very principles of our concepts of the Church.

Discussion of the first chapter of the schema showed no fundamental disagreement among the bishops. This is a biblical chapter explaining the most spiritual aspect of the Church, as scriptural metaphors and symbols describe it. It surveys the main biblical images of the Church, and happily points to the need for an elucidation of all of them—the flock, the vine, the household of God, the dwelling of the Holy Spirit, the holy city, the house of Christ, the new Eve—and not only of the Pauline image of the body of

Christ. That few divergences appeared on this biblical chapter is normal: all wish to express the way in which the Church today reads Scripture. Differences appear at the level of explanation and emphasis more than at that of reading.

The third chapter of the constitution deals with the hierarchical structure of the Church. This is a profoundly theological topic in the best sense of the term. It invites to a contemplation of the mystery of the Church, which reflects, in the relationships of its members among themselves and the organic functioning of their respective callings, the internal relations of the Blessed Trinity. Collegiality and primacy are implied in each other just as trinity and unity are implied in each other. At the level of the Church they translate the immense diversity and the deep unity of the people of God, which is as plural as it is one. Precisely at this level, we run into profound divergences among the bishops and in the Church at large. I even believe that the divergences are more profound than the debates in St. Peter's indicated at first sight. The problem is not so much to decide where the accent should be: on primacy or collegiality, on the center, the radius or the periphery. This is a secondary problem that would find an easy solution once it could be approached in a properly theological manner.

Nor is it a question of deciding now what practical institutions should best express collegiality. This is an important canonical problem, consideration of which should not interfere with the normal development of theological thought, for the development of doctrine should not be slowed down or railroaded by canonical concepts. The problem is how to think of the Church theologically when a one-sided development of Church thought, Church life and Church administration in a legalistic direction has continued for so long. Here lies the main problem of the council. The fundamental divergence has little to do with a permanent diaconate, with a married diaconate, with the sacramentality of episcopal consecration or even with the collegiality of the episcopate. Rather, it divides those who strive to consider the structure of the Church outside of canonical categories, and those who do not. The question is not to follow the rut of legal precedent; it is to analyze the current theological situation and to devise laws corresponding to it. The council, as all councils in the past, should open new avenues to law by steeping the bishops, the priests and all the Church in the word of God who speaks to us in Scripture and through the history which we call the Church's tradition.

Is this effort still possible now? Can we all proceed to the necessary catharsis of our thoughts, reactions, impressions, assumptions concerning the Church without which it is impossible to view her structure outside of the categories of power, jurisdiction and authority? Since we have all been formed, though at various times and in sundry manners, to scholastic theology and to recent canon law, and we all, in one way or another, exercise some degree of authority, and exhibit some degree of respect to the authority above us, can we still look at ourselves, at the

Church and at the laity with other than a lawyer's spectacles?

Fortunately, there are heartening indications that we still can. For the debate of the council on the nature of the Church is actually the slow and painful preparation for the eventual birth of a theological, christocentric and pastoral ecclesiology. The council has helped us to see the Church and her hierarchy in their full supernatural dimensions: the Church as the community of the children of God listening to his word and sharing the presence of his Christ; and the hierarchy as a service in justice and love for the sole glory of God.

The "new look" in the Church, then, should have the following characteristics:

First, it should be, so to speak, an ecclesiology of the cross rather than an ecclesiology of glory. In recent times, we have tended to exalt the Church above this world, emphasizing her essential relationship to Christ, who has already "overcome the world" (Jn 16:38), stressing the divinely instituted and therefore perennial elements of her structure, underlining also her aloofness from the sorry state of our universe, which she should denounce and warn against without sharing responsibility for it. Thus we have understood the notion of "mystical body of Christ" in a way which seems far removed from what St. Paul meant when he spoke of the Church as a body that is now suffering in the trials of its members: "I now supply in my flesh in the name of his body, which is the Church, to the shortcomings of the sufferings of Christ" (Col 1:24). Before showing the Church as the new Jerusalem coming down from heaven, the Book of the Apocalypse sees her as hesitant and baffled among the problems that assail the seven churches of Asia. An ecclesiology of glory makes sense only if it is balanced by an ecclesiology of the cross.

Secondly, an ecclesiology of the cross is an ecclesiology of the people, and not mainly of bishops and priests. It is an ecclesiology of the people because the people as a whole bear the brunt of the tests and trials undergone by the Church in this world. By people here I do not mean the laity alone, but all Christians, whatever their function and vocation, inasfar as they are made one people by the sacraments of Christian initiation: baptism as the access to the new creation, confirmation as the gift of the Spirit, the Eucharist as participation in the meal of thanksgiving by which the Church becomes one victim and one body with Christ. The people of God have been chosen in Christ before the foundation of the world, and have been led from Egypt, through the wilderness, toward the promised land. What happened in the Old Testament is an image of things to come, a symbol fulfilled in the paschal mystery, when we as the people of God receive the forgiveness of sins, are led through the desert of the world, are taught to hear the word, the "mystery hidden in God and now finally revealed." The Church's life on earth in our century and our country is precisely this wandering through a city of which we are not citizens, because our citizenship is in heaven, toward a city not made with hands. We are a people on pilgrimage, never resting but always ready to fold our tent and move on, unencumbered by wealth or attachments.

Thirdly, an ecclesiology of the people of God must be an ecclesiology of the kingdom. For the people on pilgrimage are led by the promise of a kingdom. Christ is "in us, the hope of glory" (Col 1:27). We are looking forward to something which is not yet with us, yet may occasionally, in times of grace, be glimpsed in anticipation. The Church is not, in the New Testament, the kingdom of God. But she has the promise of the kingdom of God, and she is, in this world, the sacrament or sign of the kingdom. The kingdom of God in which we hope is the eschatological gift of the new Jerusalem, where "God will have his dwelling with them: they will be his people, and he, God-with-them, will be their God. He will wipe away all tears from their eyes" (Ap 21:3). To an ecclesiology of the cross there corresponds the virtue of faith, by which we believe the cross of Christ to be the way to resurrection. To an ecclesiology of the people there corresponds love, by which we share all things in the communion of saints and we are made organically one. To an ecclesiology of the kingdom there corresponds hope, which sustains us in the knowledge that the sufferings of this life are nothing, compared to the glory to come.

What concrete forms these emphases in our theology of the Church should take, I do not know. The current concern should be to steep ourselves in this total view of the Church, replacing our excessively canonical concepts by more theological ideas. It is not to devise new regulations, new rubrics or new organizations. These may come in their own good time. Yet they cannot be effective in any way unless we are prepared, and we have prepared others, to know and understand the Church better, unless we have experienced her, and we have given others the experience of her, as the communion of man with man in Christ and for him, at the service of the purpose of God over the universe.

8 THE ECUMENICAL DIMENSION

Ecumenism has been brought to the attention of the Church at large by the apparent permanence of divisions which all sides hoped would be transitory when they broke out in the eleventh and the sixteenth centuries. It is the intention of Jesus Christ that his disciples should be one, "so that the world may believe." The apostle Paul understood this oneness of the body, persisting and growing through the ages, to be a manifestation of the fullness of Christ, "through whom all beings are reconciled for him, on earth as in heaven" (Col 1:20). For St. John also, Christ is the one who alone is "full of grace and truth," "of whose fullness we all have received, grace on grace" (Jn 1:14, 16). There is therefore no grace outside of his unity. And yet the Christian world, spiritually and institutionally divided, has been offering for centuries the spectacle of self-contradiction: it has continued preaching the message of unity, but it has done it in a state of disunion.

Because the problem of Christian reunion has, in recent decades, been forced on the attention of Christians by circumstances, ecumenism has come to mean, for most of us, a special approach to separated Christians. Ecumenism,

the manifestation of the *oecumene* or universality to
which the Church must be adequate, is an attempt to restore the broken unity of Christendom in order to bring it
up to what we believe to be the unbroken unity of the
Church. As far as it goes, this is correct, but it is not complete. Before ecumenism can be developed as an attitude,
ecumenicity must be understood as a basic dimension of
Christianity. Ecumenism will bring to light what ecumenicity is in the mystery of the Church.

Theological reflection on ecumenicity should lead us to
grasp the practical requirements of ecumenism and the
special function of the laity in relation to it.

It has happened to all of us to discover in ourselves
depths of which we were unaware before. There are times
when the gates of perception within us open, and a new
interior universe is revealed. We penetrate beyond a veil.
We discover that what appeared to us as the limit of our
self is actually an opening on a wider self. We find unknown
dimensions in our existence and unexhausted possibilities
in our life. Where we believed ourselves constrained and
restricted by our surroundings, our history, our moral and
intellectual shortcomings, we now know that beyond our
first frontier there stretches another; that our soul builds
layers and layers around its center and that this center itself recedes as we reach deeper toward it. This may have
happened to me when I was contemplating a painting: new
aspects of reality appeared through the canvas. It may have

happened as I was listening to a symphony and the strains of the music carried me into spiritual realms that I had never known. It may have happened as I was reading Hegel and I looked up new philosophical vistas. In each of these cases, new sensations and perceptions have occasioned an intuition of being as being. A shock has been given to my spirit which has impelled it toward new spiritual experiences, and, beyond appearances, I have seen reality. This intuition of being is the essence of esthetic experience and philosophical insight.

What have I thus discovered about life? Life has the dimension of estrangement, for we are all separated one from another; and it has the dimension of reconciliation, for from the shore of my consciousness I attempt to communicate with the shore of your consciousness on the other side of the ocean. Life is both shores and it is also the ocean itself between us, which imposes discontinuity and makes continuity possible, which separates and unites us, for we can communicate only through the space that keeps us apart. I have discovered this infinity of life, which embosoms not only myself and the friend whom I love and from whom I remain separated, but all men and all things. There is in life an infinite of estrangement and an infinite of reconciliation, the endless pulsing of concentration and expansion, of recoiling into oneself and reaching out toward the universe of men and of things. Thus all that is alive is a center desiring to reach as far as the total circumference of life. Life in me stretches out in an endeavor to be one with life in my friends coming to me, and with life in all things, known and unknown, potentially inclined toward me. Life is an effort of the particular to be one with the universal. The universe, the *oecumene*, the whole world, is what I desire. Life has the dimension of ecumenicity, in which estrangement and reconciliation are not alternate choices, but simultaneous conditions enabling each to desire all and to be united with all.

Thus ecumenicity appears as a dimension of life, by which the life of each particular being implicitly contains, in hope at least, the life of all other beings. It is a universal openness, an exchange between man and man, a shuttling between being and being, the weaving of an invisible woof by which each being relates himself to all others in what, in ultimate analysis, must be love. If this is a dimension of natural life, how much more must it not be a dimension of supernatural life?

Christianity is the advent of true man. Once in human history there appeared a man who was, by his hypostatic union to the Word of God, totally open to the full dimension of ecumenicity. "God was in Christ, reconciling the world to himself" (2 Cor 5:19). In Christ estrangement between being and being was overcome by reconciliation. He communicated with the dead to bring them back to life, with the fig tree to order it to wither, with the storm to make it subside, with the sick to heal them, with the sinners to forgive them. His coming was the fullness of time. To his dying the cosmos associated itself, sending earthquakes and darkness in the middle of the day. His birth brought together angels and shepherds, and his death opened paradise to a dying thief, to all dying thieves. All this is true of the man Jesus and of him alone, because he is the Word made flesh. "All things were made by him, and without him there was nothing. What was made was life in him" (Jn 1:3–4). Or, with St. Paul, let us say: "He has elected us in Christ before the foundation of the world to be saints and blameless in his presence in love" (Eph 1:4). Or, as he says in the Apocalypse: "I am alpha and omega, the first and the last, the principle and the consummation . . . I am the root of the race of David, the radiant morning star" (Ap 22:16).

To be baptized in his name is to become a new creature, to acquire a new being, to be a new man. "Christ in you, hope of glory," St. Paul tells the Colossians (1:27), that is, by being reconciled with God through the new creation we have the hope of reconciliation with all men and all things, of partaking in the cosmic liturgy which forms the glory of God. The radiant morning star appears at the dawn of a new day, the day when universal estrangement between being and being, between man and man, between man and God, will be absorbed in universal reconciliation. The ecumenical dimension of Christian life is the expectation and the anticipation, in faith and in hope, of the day of reconciliation, which we may boldly describe by appropriating a genial vision of Karl Marx: in Christ alone, shall we say, is "the positive abolition of human self-alienation . . . the definitive resolution of the antagonism between man and nature and between man and man . . . the true solution of the conflict between existence and essence, between objectification and self-affirmation, between freedom and necessity, between individual and species . . . the solution of the riddle of history."[1]

Christianity is the faith that such an event took place when the Word of God was born of the Virgin Mary as Jesus of Nazareth. It is also the accession of man, in faith and through the sacraments of faith, to the freedom of the children of God. It is, too, the opening of mankind as a whole, and of the cosmos that supports it, to a participation in the new creation, through the institution of the Church which is here and now the structure and the first-fruits of the new creation; which is already, in anticipation, the new heaven and the new earth: "For the creature in expectation," St. Paul proclaims, "longs for the revelation of the children of God. It was made the victim of frustration not by its own choice, but because of him who made it so, with the hope that the universe itself is to be freed from the shackles of mortality and enter upon the liberty and splendor of the children of God. We know that all creation to this day groans and is in travail" (Rom 8:19–21).

In traditional language, *catholicity* is the mark of the Church as the fullness of Christ present on earth, among men, in the highways and by-ways of society, in the lanes and the slums of the human city. "I believe in one, holy, catholic and apostolic Church." This means, I believe the Church to be the total presence of Christ, Savior and Lord,

[1] Quoted by Erich Fromm in *Marx's Concept of Man*, New York 1961, 127.

the realm of redemption, the channel of salvation, the only access to freedom and love, the sole solution to the dilemmas of mankind. This catholicity implies two other marks, or has two complementary aspects. *Collegiality* is the cohesion of the Church with herself, the unanimity of her members, pastors and laymen, the dialogic process by which the separate members of the Church reach and formulate her mind in unity. And *ecumenicity* is the orientation of the Church toward mankind and toward the cosmos, speaking to them the word of salvation and listening to the voices which express, in ambiguous terms, the millennial expectation of the universe for the manifestation of the children of God. Ecumenicity implies a hidden correspondence between the structure of the Church, her tension toward the second advent and the fulfillment of salvation, and the structure of the universe, its tension toward the end of its evolution.

In this wide perspective, ecumenism, as an activity of Christians, is implied in ecumenicity. Whereas catholicity is a datum, ecumenicity is a progress. Catholicity is at the start of the Church, as a divine gift already given; ecumenicity is, ultimately, at the completion of the Church's task on earth, as a divine gift still to be given, present with us in hope, but not totally in act until the second coming of Christ manifests the total identity between the Church and the universe. If Catholicism is the system of thought and life in which we try to embody the catholicity of the Church, ecumenism is a program of thought and life by which we strive to bring her ecumenicity to light.

At this point, the theological reflection which we are out-
lining returns to the fact of a disunited Christendom.
Ecumenism, as was said at the beginning of this chapter,
has developed over the last two centuries as a way to heal
the schisms of Christians. This is not accidental. It corresponds to the basic structure of ecumenicity. The ecumenicity of the Church requires that the Church as a whole
open a dialogue with mankind. The cosmos has found its
spokesman in man himself, who is the voice of the universe.
It is mankind which, through its scientists, scrutinizes the
complexities of nature; through its explorers has seen the
geography of the earth and has begun to launch its space-
ships toward the planets to look with human eyes on the
cosmography; through its poets sings the tragedies and the
beauties of creation; through its philosophers interprets the
world; through its planners and politicians organizes itself.
The movement by which the Church wishes to embrace all
creation necessarily goes through all mankind. But mankind cannot take the Church seriously as long as it cannot
see her as a whole rather than as a fissiparous collection of
separated Christian bodies. The oneness which Catholics
see in their Church is visible to no one else. To all others,
Christianity looks not like one Church surrounded by a
few eccentric chapels, but like a multitude of competing
organizations. Christian unity is thus a requirement of the
conversion of the world.

What we can thus state as the conclusion of the preced-
ing analysis corresponds exactly to the Gospel. The Lord
prayed: "May they all be one: as you, Father, are in me

and I in you, so also may they be in us, that the world may
believe that you did send me" (Jn 17:21). And: "The
world will know that you are my disciples, in that you have
love for one another" (Jn 13:35). The unity of Christians
is a condition for their effective dialogue with mankind.
The conversion of mankind has been promised as the fulfillment of Christianity's inner unity, as the consequence
and the reflection, in the world as a whole, of the radiation
coming from the Church, seen, by mankind, as the one
and only realm of salvation.

A look at the history of the Church would show that
this was not a vain promise, or a mistaken fear that Christian disunion would hamper the spread of the Gospel. The
great missionary eras of the Catholic Church preceded the
rise of Protestantism or took place, like the missionary saga
in Latin America, or the early missionary penetration of
China and India, in areas where the recent upheaval of
Protestantism had no influence. As soon as Protestantism
organized its own missions, another phase began: from that
time on, Christian missionaries have appeared as rivals.
There have been many conversions, but hardly corresponding to the sum total of efforts and sacrifices made to send
and support the missions. And this very day, when all the
churches of disunited Christendom are burning with missionary zeal, we can see the handwriting on the wall. For
one African convert to Christianity, ten are converted to
Islam. The number of births in India each year is approximately equal to the number of Christians in that country,
which is to say that Indian Christianity is, in proportion

to the total population, dwindling. In China Christianity is being wiped out. Several Asian and African countries, such as Ceylon and the Sudan, are severely restricting the movements of missionaries and native clergy. And traditionally Christian areas, Catholic and Protestant alike, worship not indeed the God of Abraham, Isaac and Jacob, but the god of comfort and the divine dollar. "He who has ears to hear, let him hear what the Spirit is telling the Churches" (Ap 2:7). He who has eyes to see, let him read the mysterious script on the broken walls of Christian unity.

At this crucial point in the history of his Church, God has raised a Pope who has called for a new approach to our problem, an approach which is not, like that of the now dying Counter-reformation, one of piecemeal conquest, but, like that of the early Church, one of "total confrontation." By "total confrontation" I mean that the need is no longer to defend some tenets of doctrine with persuasive arguments. It is rather to present Christianity as a coherent whole fully adequate to the needs, the desires, the implications, the experiences, the tragedies, the hopes, of mankind as a whole. The question is no longer to convert one village or one tribe, one province or one country; it is to convert the world. In this respect, I believe that John XXIII renewed beyond the recent tradition of the Counter-reformation, with the older tradition of patristic times and the middle ages, with what I would call the "classical" concept of the Church's function and activity. A few months before the council opened, the late Pontiff told an audience: "What must first of all be manifested, always in all things and by all, is the sense of catholicity and universality in faith." In other words, the totality of the Church must now face the world's problems. This is no time anymore for narrow outlooks; we cannot afford to be provincial or parochial; the prospects for the Church can no longer be gauged at the national or the continental level. We are reaching a more basic issue and we are beginning to see a more apocalyptic vision: the Church must prepare herself to be totally accepted or totally rejected. Pope Paul hinted at this undertaking in the closing remarks of his address to the fathers assembled for the second session:

From the window of the council, opened wide on the world, the Church . . . looks toward men of culture and learning, scientists, artists. . . . The Church is concerned for workers. . . . The Church looks to the leaders of the people. . . . And then the Catholic Church looks further still, beyond the confines of the Christian horizon. For how can she put limits to her love . . . ?

The repristination initiated by John XXIII and carried on by Paul VI is therefore not simply a "return to the sources." It is this indeed, but also much more. It implies a return to the Gospel, as presented in holy Scripture and as explained in the Church's multicentennial tradition. But it requires also something which is infinitely arduous, a spiritual renovation of Christian life. The Second Vatican Council is, in the words of John XXIII, not only "a great testimony to what the Good Shepherd is," but also "a

quest after his essential features." This was said in a homily
for the feast of Pentecost (June 10, 1962) which constitutes,
in my opinion, the most revealing document of this great
Pontiff. What are the features of the Good Shepherd which
we need to recover? They correspond to the purpose of his
pastoral care, which is sanctification, understood in the
widest possible sense. Through the sacraments of the
Church, as Pope John said, "all is sanctified; man is
sanctified from the beginning to the end of his earthly
pilgrimage and in all his activities, both individual and
collective." Then, in a vision of what the Church ought to
be, the Pope continued:

The Church follows in the footsteps of the Good Shepherd
in his mystical pilgrimage from village to village, from house
to house. She leaves the enclosure of her cenacles and, imitat-
ing her divine founder and witnessing to him, she walks along
all the roads of the world. She cannot contain the fervor of the
continual Pentecost that invades her and inspires her to lead
the flock toward the rich pastures of eternal life. Such is the
mission of the catholic and apostolic Church: to gather all
men, whom selfishness and weariness could keep apart . . . The
Church is not surprised that men do not immediately understand her language and that they are tempted to restrict the
perfect code of individual salvation and of social progress to
the limited horizons of their personal life and interests . . .
Guardian of the truth, she wants to enter all and to obtain the
grace of sanctifying all, in familial, national and international
circles.

This is a message of spiritual liberation, of grandeur, of
generosity, based on the conviction that the Church, in her
catholicity, is ultimately larger than the world and has to

compensate, by her openness on the spiritual, for the claustrophobia of a universe limiting its vision to material horizons. Such is the dimension of ecumenicity, an implicit dimension of all life, which is all the more essential to Christians as Christ, in whom we live, is the Pantocrator, the Lord of all things, who, after he assumed the form of the servant, was "exalted and given the Name which is above every name" (Phil 2:9).

Ecumenism is the activity tending to promote and develop the ecumenicity of the Church. I shall not go into details as to the functions of the layman in this field; I shall only point out several indispensable principles which must be at the basis of his action.

By his baptism, the Christian layman has been initiated into a universal order, an order with universal claims and scope. He has been made a witness to the cosmic function of Christ, in whom all men and all things find their place. By his reception of the Eucharist, he has been united to the one "through whom all things were made." The first thing to do, then, is to develop in us this sense of the universal mission of Christ and of his Church, the sense of catholicity, of ecumenicity, so that we may always choose a large, universal, generous point of view rather than a small, local, selfish one. We must enlarge our soul to understand the views and purposes of the Lord. We must never judge and appreciate the Church from the standpoint of our little parish, but from that of the universal Church. To restrict

the Church's problems and tasks to those of our parish is
the best way to misunderstand our times and its spiritual
requirements. On the contrary, local problems, in order to
find their solution, must be seen in the light of the universal Church. The meaning of the Second Vatican Council
must not be gauged from its possible influence on the
financing of schools; rather schools themselves must find
their relatively small place in the light of a spiritual interpretation of our century. What we need therefore is a spiritual transformation, what Pope John, addressing a congress
of Austrian Catholics, has called "a true interior renovation
of yourselves, an ever more really and deeply Christian life
in the Spirit of Jesus Christ," this Spirit who, as the Pope
wrote in the same letter, "must be a leaven at all the levels
of the society which is now being constructed."

Spiritual does not mean discarnate. Christian spirituality
is essentially enfleshed. An ecumenical attitude does not
remain an abstraction, a theory or a vague ideal. It is a
reality to be expressed in the realities of our daily life. The
layman's participation in the Church's life is first of all
liturgical. The Church is always the Church in prayer, expressing the word of God in the traditional forms of its
worship. The main school of generosity, where we learn to
open our souls to God, is liturgical prayer. There are too
many instances in which our prayer closes our mind rather
than opens it, because we come to it with an individualistic
point of view, in a basically selfish frame of mind, with our
own attachment to our own formulas, praying in separation
from the spiritual intentions of the Church and the cor-

porate forms of its worship, in what is, in a word, an implicitly schismatic attitude. The result was called by John XXIII "an impoverishment of worship, a disproportion and a disharmony." The Pope therefore invited all, in his own words, "to make the meaning and the method of their prayer ever more universal." Thus does the liturgical constitution say (no. 26):

Liturgical services are not private functions, but are celebrations of the Church, which is the "sacrament of unity," namely the holy people united and ordered under their bishops. Therefore liturgical services pertain to the whole body of the Church; they manifest it and have effects upon it; but they concern the individual members of the Church in different ways, according to their differing rank, office and actual participation.

This implies that the laity today—whatever the local clergy does or does not do—ought to take an active part in the liturgical renewal of Christian life, to promote an active participation in the liturgy, to request from their priests —as is their right—sermons or homilies where they may hear the Gospel preached and find true spiritual elevation.

Since ecumenicity is the Church's adequacy to mankind and the universe, there cannot be a spiritual renewal of Christian life without a sympathetic identification of ourselves with all mankind. The Christian layman must thrive to outgrow all sectarian mentality, to think and to love on the scale of the Church in her widest catholicity. We should have the generosity of mind which recognizes, with John XXIII, that "wherever in the world there are honest and God-fearing men, these men, knowingly or

not, assist in some way the advent of the kingdom of God."
A general acknowledgement of this elementary truth will
occasion changes in our apostolic methods. The ecumenical
movement has already required a new approach to separated
Christians, one very different from the polemics and the
apologetics of yesterday. As noted above, the missionary
situation is urging us to take a new look at the general problem of the Church's mission and to develop a strategy of
total confrontation. The liturgical movement is slowly bringing back our practices of piety and the expression of our worship to biblical and patristic standards, away from the decadence of the last centuries. The Second Vatican Council
is a meeting point of all these movements of awakening,
what Pope Paul has called "a new spring, a reawakening
of the mighty spiritual and moral energies that at present
lie dormant." The council fathers have already invited us
to prepare for and participate in these new forms of Catholic life. In chapter 2 of the Constitution on the Sacred
Liturgy (no. 48), we read:

The Church, therefore, earnestly desires that Christ's faithful, when present at this mystery of faith [the eucharistic sacri-
fice], should not be there as strangers or silent spectators; on
the contrary, through a good understanding of the rites and
prayers they should take part in the sacred action, conscious of
what they are doing, with devotion and full collaboration. They
should be instructed by God's word and be nourished at the
table of the Lord's body; they should give thanks to God; by
offering the immaculate victim, not only through the hands of
the priest, but also with him, they should learn also to offer
themselves; through Christ the Mediator, they should be

drawn day by day into ever more perfect union with God and with each other, so that finally God may be all in all.

The duty of Christian laymen, therefore, is not to be satisfied with old forms of apostolate or church organization; without undue love of novelty, but with an acute sense of the requirements of modern times, they must contribute to the spiritual modernization of the Church.

Finally, it should go without saying that we cannot make the necessary effort to adapt the Church to the changing circumstances of the world unless we deeply feel our commitment to mankind and to the world. Nobody will take us seriously if our public theoretical statements are not matched by our daily practical behavior. It is significant that Pope John once described the purpose of the council: "that man's sojourn on earth be less sad." When we read this, let us not hasten to conclude that the late Pontiff was endorsing the prologue to the American constitution listing the "pursuit of happiness" as an elementary right of man! In the context of pontifical thought, the sadness in question is a much deeper anguish than can be remedied by the "pursuit of happiness" as commonly understood. It is the anguish of the Christian before the persecutions that assail the Church, the anguish of man before the disorders and hatreds of the world, before senseless strife and hopeless violence. Before this sadness we have no right to continue in what Pope John called "inert indifferentism." We cannot shun the most flagrant instance of those things that make our world a sad world and life a sad experience: the refusal to treat man as man, to identify oneself with every man regardless of color or race. The socialization of which Pope John spoke in his encyclical *Mater et Magistra* is ultimately the impossibility today of judging individual behavior with the narrow standard of individuals, and the correlative necessity of seeing each of our actions as a social gesture with significance and consequences, not only for the man who sees me, but also for mankind that does not see me. The ecumenical function of the layman implies his ability and willingness to espouse the just cause of every other man.

I began by trying to show that ecumenicity is a dimension of life—and if of life, then much more so of supernatural life. It will be a fitting conclusion to remark that the practice of ecumenism, in the sense it has been defined, is also life-giving. The opening of our soul to the works of God in mankind and the universe will inescapably attune us to the magnificence of God himself. We cannot be united to the least of Christ's brethren without being thereby united to Christ. We cannot love and contemplate his created glory without loving and contemplating him. While ecumenism will make us more human, it will also give us more awareness of the dimensions of the lordship of Christ, King of the universe.

9 THE TWO FACES OF UNITY

The search for religious unity is one of the important phenomena in the history of modern Christianity. In the words of Gustave Weigel, it is "the most striking ecclesiological event since the sixteenth century Reformation." Contrary to what could have been expected when it began, this search has been lasting. It was not the passing fancy or the unsubstantial dream of a few idealists. It corresponds to the deepest desires of the religious soul and, which is significant, to the general longing of our time for unity. This search for unity may be said to be the center of twentieth century concerns. *The Unity of Philosophical Experience* is not only the title of a book by Étienne Gilson: it is the intention behind most modern philosophies. In their different ways, Marxism and existentialism both aspire to the unity of subject and object in which philosophy would find the ultimate unity of experience. The logical positivism of British and American empiricists would seem to escape this concern for unity. Yet even there, one feels the desire for one formula covering all logical processes. In science the search for one formula which would be explanatory of the universe is clear. And Teilhard de Chardin has rendered the immense service of relating this search to religious concerns, so that ultimately physical and chemical reactions find their meaning and their link in the evolution of mankind toward one goal, its unity with itself through its union to God.

In one sense, then, all these movements are quests for religious unity. Philosophical experience has immediately religious implications. The underlying unity of scientific phenomena points to the religious dimension of the universe. We should not make undue inferences from the scientific vision of the world to its religious vision. Yet, starting from the religious vision, we have to say with Karl Heim: "If God exists, then our gaze must be directed to the whole of the universe with all that it comprises. For God is the omnipresent Creator and Lord, who controls the rotation of the galaxies just as he controls the circling of the electrons within the atom."[1] And even the quest for political unity is a testimony to the human existential drive for what Paul Tillich calls "the Reunion of the separated."[2] It is an attempt to overcome the estrangement of existence.

This universal quest has found a privileged field in the ecumenical movement. The ecumenical movement in its contemporary form may be dated from the year 1910, when the Missionary Conference of Edinburgh marked the starting point of the efforts to establish a world organization of Christian churches. This took two successive forms. First, it was a matter of grouping together individual Christians

[1] *Christian Faith and Natural Sciences*, New York 1957, 30.
[2] *Love, Power, and Justice*, New York 1960, 25.

desirous of promoting religious unity. Thus the "Faith and Order Movement" and the "Life and Work Movement" worked on more or less parallel lines, between the end of the First World War and the beginning of the Second World War. This period between the wars was fruitful in that many Protestant and Orthodox leaders acquired experience in the field of relations with other Christians. Yet there was a weak point at the basis of both movements. The problem of Christian unity does not exist so much at the individual as at the corporate level. Divisions between Christians are breaches of charity on the part of the individuals. They are failures to carry out the implications of Christian life, but they are also more tragic than that. They are failures at the level of the structure of the Church, involving the Church as a whole and resulting in the existence of rival communities. To envision the ecumenical movement only as a movement of individuals could be only a first step. It was soon followed by a second step. In 1937, the two movements of Faith and Order and of Life and Work decided to disappear in order to create a new movement at the level of the Christian communities themselves. The formation of the World Council of Churches was the outcome: it is an organization not of individuals, but of churches seeking to promote unity.

Two concerns have thus successively dominated the ecumenical movement. The first was a concern for the spontaneity of life, as manifested in prophetic individuals, disturbed by Christian disunion and endeavoring to prepare for reunion. The second was for the structure of the

churches as such: the ecumenical movement cannot succeed, or so it seems, without a rediscovery of the unifying
structure of the Christian community. The churches themselves must seek for unity in order to find themselves and
to find each other in the Church. Since the formation of the
World Council, the second concern dominates, though it
has not superseded the former. Both coexist in ecumenical
circles today.

The movement toward religious unity has something to
do with the structure of the church, and also something to
do with the life of people in the church. Starting from the
second point of view, the Protestants who launched the
ecumenical movement felt it necessary to introduce the
first also in their preoccupations, and even to make it predominant. In the words of W. A. Visser 't Hooft, "radical
changes in thought and structure will have to take place
before our churches will again be truly responsive to the
divine call."[3] From the point of view of Catholic theology,
this is extremely important. The main difference between
Protestant and Catholic approaches to the reform of the
church lies in this notion of structure. The Catholic tradition has always been eager to reform the life of the
church, that is, to purify the faith and the ethics of her
members; but she has always refused to reform the structure of the church.

The structure of the church, that is, the episcopal-
sacramental hierarchy, is God-given. It is the divine-human

[3] *Our Ecumenical Task in the Light of History*, New York 1960,
15.

framework for the life of the church. Life may be reformed, whereas structure is irreformable. Through it, the Church partakes in the permanence of God; by it she is already an eschatological reality, anticipating on and participating in the stability of life in God. One of the conditions of a Catholic reform is therefore "to remain in the communion of the whole."[4] The whole in question is precisely the God-given structure.

The Protestant movements of reform, in the past, overlooked this requirement of a Catholic reformation. Thus Luther and Calvin were led to define the church as the society "where the word is truly preached and the sacraments truly administered." This was placing the church on the prophetical level of life, without mentioning the institutional level of structure. It could not do full justice to the biblical conception of the communion of God with man, in which both prophetic discontinuity and priestly continuity are essential to the people of God. The former results from grace, which inspires holiness in those whom God has chosen. The latter manifests the permanence of the presence of God in the Church his bride. Structure is the image of the second Person of the Trinity, and corresponds to the permanence of his incarnation. Life refers us to the third Person: "The Spirit breathes where he will, and no one knows where it goes or whence it comes" (Jn 3:8).

The contemporary movement of Protestantism toward religious unity tries to restore this structural dimension.

[4] Yves Congar, *True and False Reform in the Church*, New York 1951, 146.

Catholic theology should therefore interpret it as a movement away from the ecclesiological discontinuity of the Protestant reformers, toward a recovery of the structural wholeness and framework which God has given his church without ever repenting his gift. From this standpoint, the ecumenical movement today differs from several attempts that were made in the past to restore religious unity. Two kinds of attempts, made in opposite directions, may be briefly described.

In 1809 Thomas Campbell, an ex-Presbyterian minister, published a *Declaration and Address* in which he asserted that "the church of Christ upon earth is essentially, intentionally and constitutionally one, consisting of all those in every place that profess their faith in Christ and obedience to Him in all things according to the Scriptures, and that manifest the same by their tempers and conduct."[5] His son, Alexander Campbell, soon took over the leadership of this nondenominational movement, which wanted to be a return to the simplicity of primitive Christianity and a restoration of the church as founded by Christ through a renunciation of all denominational features. The Disciples of Christ "belong to no sect, but only to Christ's church."[6] As recently as 1946, a "Commission on Restudy of the Disciples of Christ," set up by the International Convention of the Disciples, listed the following basic principles: "The unity of Christians according to the program and prayer of

[5] Ronald Osborn, "Disciples of Christ," *The American Church of the Protestant Heritage*, ed. Vergilius Ferm, 393.
[6] Op. cit. 406

our Lord, with Christ himself the center of that unity, by the restoration of New Testament Christianity, is necessary to the realization of God's program for human redemption."[7] In other words, the Disciples wished to be not a denomination, but "one with the church which was founded on the day of Pentecost and is set forth in the New Testament."[8] They were born of an ecumenical purpose. They tried to carry out Thomas Campbell's dream of a reunion of all the true disciples of Christ beyond and outside all restrictive denominations. Such was their purpose. Yet it is clear even to the casual onlooker that, since about 1830, the Disciples of Christ have constituted a new denomination. This attempt to unite all Christians has actually divided them more than they were before.

It would seem obvious that one cause of this failure was precisely the very purpose which they set out to fulfill. The Campbells and their friends wanted a nondenominational Christianity, which nothing but the New Testament would determine. They wanted a Christianity of *life*, marked by "faith in Christ and obedience to Him," and manifested "by their tempers and conduct." One could not express more strongly the concern for Christian *life* which motivated them. But the life which they envisioned was totally without structure. When they rejected denominational status, they fell into a trap. Not only did they overlook the fact that the church of the New Testament has a hierarchical structure; they also believed that life could last

[7] Op. cit. 407–408
[8] Op. cit. 405

without structure. Yet structure, which was intentionally discarded, returned with a vengeance. The Disciples form today a denomination that has failed in its ecumenical purpose. Although some may still refuse the term "denomination," they nonetheless constitute a single Protestant community.

The lesson to be learned is clear: Christian unity can neither be preserved nor be restored without an institutional framework. In the absence of a God-given framework, another one, man-made, will be substituted. This is a clear instance of the necessary correlation between life and structure, between spirit and institution. This ecumenical attempt failed precisely because of a total lack of concern for structure.

Other attempts were made, in the past, to restore unity. Some of them failed not because of lack of concern for structure, but because of lack of concern for life. Twice already, the Catholic and the Orthodox churches, after their schism of 1054, have reunited. In 1274 at the Second Council of Lyons, and in 1439 at the Council of Florence, the acts of union were written, agreed on and signed by the spiritual and temporal leaders of the churches. The liturgy was solemnly celebrated together as an act of thanksgiving and as a manifestation of the restored unity of eastern and western Catholicity. Reunion was effected from the point of view of the structure of church. It was negotiated by bishops as responsible for their flocks; it was accepted by them in the name of the Church over which they presided in the Holy Spirit. Yet in neither case did the union last. It was broken again a few years later, under the pressure of the monks and people of Constantinople. In this case, account had been taken of the structure of the church; but the leaders on both sides had forgotten or dismissed the imponderable elements of life. They had forgotten that the structure of the church must keep pace with the spontaneous religiosity and the instinctive reaction of the people. The structure of the church is not without content; the hierarchy does not exist without the laity. When they are oblivious of this fact, the representatives of the church's structure, that is, the bishops, can only find that the life of the people in the church is not following them. The church does not exist only as a structure; it is a structure rooted in the life of the Christian people.

Failure to take account of this doomed the reunions between Orthodox and Catholics in the thirteenth and the fifteenth centuries. Lack of concern for life and spontaneity can only cause the structure of the church to turn, as it were, in a void.

The first mistake lies at the door of Protestantism, which is more concerned for life than for structure. Its dreams see unity as a spontaneous union of all that believe in Christ, and tend to understress the necessity of the church's structure. Thus new denominations are born out of attempts at unity which eventually fail because of their wish to be free of denominational ties.

The second mistake is the perpetual temptation of Catholics, who are prone to think of unity in terms of falling into a pattern (the Catholic pattern) and giving allegiance to a structure (the Catholic structure). They may, at the same time, forget that unity must also be the unity of a Christian with his Lord in the mystery of grace; they may omit the preparations at the level of Christian life without which a structural reunion cannot hope to last; they tend to think of conversion as an official acknowledgement of authority, forgetting sometimes that it must also be a conversion of the heart.

In the light of these lessons from the remote and recent past, it would seem that the future of the movements toward religious unity lies in their being able to steer clear of both abysses. They must disregard neither life nor structure. They must search for a lasting structure of church union while knowing that no structure will guarantee unity unless this unity has been desired, prayed for and accepted in the hearts of all Christians. A structure without life is a skeleton without flesh; and life without structure is amorphous and spineless, lacking the vitality that can only come from a framework.

Precisely, the World Council of Churches has tried to avoid both excesses, even though it has approached the question of structure with the utmost diffidence.

The ecumenical movement in Protestantism arose out of the life of Protestant Christianity: the drive for union appears as an exigency of life. Starting from life, it has largely become a search for a corresponding structure. It is true that the various denominations have been drawn toward either of these two poles of ecclesiology. There are, as seen by Visser 't Hooft, "pietist traditions," which stress and perhaps overstress life, and "church-centered traditions," which are more interested in structure. The task of the ecumenical movement appears to be a conciliation of these two tendencies. Thus Visser 't Hooft sees it: both traditions "are very much alive and still have a mission to perform . . . The tradition which makes the Church central is of decisive importance in our present situation. We need to be told again and again that the Church of Christ *exists* and that our task is to participate in the manifestation of its holiness and unity. At the same time, the tradition which we have called pietist has still an important message for us. Its historic mission is to remind the Church of the simple truth that the Gospel begins with a call to repentance, *metanoia*, that is, "turning around, returning to the Lord . . . Now these two traditions of ecumenical thought and life need each other. The task of our generation is to seek to achieve their integration, so that they may correct and strengthen each other."[9] The two strains are very clear in this text. The task of integration will not be easy, precisely because the two traditions have developed far apart from each other. It will be all the more arduous as even the most church-centered traditions in Protestantism are still seeking for a structure with universal validity. The Archbishop of Canterbury, William Temple, put the problem of a universal structure forcefully: "I firmly believe in the Holy Catholic Church, and I am sincerely sorry that it does not

[9] Visser 't Hooft, op. cit. 12–13.

exist."[10] Yet it is from this seeming absence of a universal Christian structure that the movement toward Christian unity has started in a search for structure.

The World Council does not claim to provide such a structure. It is important to realize the relationship between the Council, the churches or denominations, and *the church*, as it is seen from within the Council itself.

The constitution of the World Council, as adopted at the first assembly at Amsterdam in 1948, expressly emphasized life rather than structure in the pattern of the Council's activities and therefore in the nature of the Council: "While earnestly seeking fellowship in thought and action for all its members, the Council disavows any thought of becoming a single unified church structure independent of the churches which have joined in constituting the Council, or a structure dominated by a centralized administrative authority."[11] The first part of this sentence expresses the Council's concern for life (fellowship); the second part staves off a possible identification of the Council with the structure of unity which is being sought. Yet it was hoped that the existence of the Council had ecclesiological implications. And as soon as we say *ecclesia*, the assembly, the congregation, the people of God, we inevitably introduce structural categories. The church cannot be thought of meaningfully without a reference to its structural elements.

Yet because we are, in the present state of the World

[10] I find myself unable to locate this quotation; however I feel quite sure the quote is correct.

[11] "Toronto Statement," *The First Six Years, 1948–1954,* 114.

Council, in a Protestant-dominated atmosphere, the Toronto statement, in July 1950, avoided overstress on structure. It took care in the first place to do away with the
dark suspicion, in some Protestant quarters, that the
Council was on the way to impose a new church structure
on its members. On the contrary, the Council "is not a
super-church. It is not the world church. It is not the
Una Sancta of which the Creed speaks. This misunderstanding arises again and again although it has been denied
as clearly as possible in official pronouncements of the
Council."[12] Official pronouncements are one thing: the
need for structure is another. Official pronouncements do
not deny the need, but only the right of the Council to
impose such a structure. Yet those who are over concerned
for life at the expense of structure are likely to interpret
every attempt to organize life as the imposition of a structure. The situation of the Council, which sees the need
for a structure, without which life cannot last, yet which
does not see what shape that structure can take, is well
expressed in the two following points. On the one hand,
"the Council stands for church unity." On the other, no
conception of church unity "can be called the ecumenical
theory."[13]

This official toning down of the structural elements of
church unity might seem to imply that the Council ex-
clusively relates itself to the life of those who seek unity,

[12] Op. cit. 114.
[13] Op. cit. 116.

while it would avoid any commitment to a church structure. But this would be a false assumption, for the two points of view of life and structure are well balanced toward the end of the Toronto statement: "It is the common teaching of the churches that the church as the temple of God is at the same time a building which has been built and a building which is being built. The church has, therefore, aspects which belong to its very structure and essence and cannot be changed. But it has other aspects, which are subject to change. Thus the life of the church, as it expresses itself in its witness to its own members and to the world, needs constant renewal."[14] In other words, the structure of the church is God-given, and therefore unchanging and improving. The Council sees its task mainly in terms of life: it helps the churches to enter into "a mutual exchange of thought and experience."[15] And it does not know for sure what unchanging structure God has given his church. It does not decide between "church-centered" traditions and pietistic traditions, yet it holds the goal of their integration before the eyes of its member-churches. This comes to mean that it hopes that the unchanging structure of the church will some day be manifested by God. It encourages the churches to seek for structure in order to improve life. But this search for structure is periodically dampened by an overwhelming fear that structure should stifle life.

This fear has been manifested on several occasions

[14] Op. cit. 118–119.
[15] Op. cit. 119

since the Toronto statement was published. In 1958, Visser 't Hooft published an article on "The Super-Church and the Ecumenical Movement."[16] These twenty pages gave instances of super-church behavior in the past history of the church (mainly of the Roman Catholic Church). Super-church behavior is the stifling of the elements of *life* by an overpowering structure. Indeed this concern should remain with ecumenists today. Yet at times some give the impression of having more than a concern about the possibility of choking life. A sort of super-church complex seems to dominate some quarters. This would become dangerous if it pushed the ecumenical movement into a denial of the need to channel the energies of life into a guiding and supporting structure. In one of his books,[17] Visser 't Hooft takes the doctrine of St. Vincent of Lerins on tradition as the very type of stagnation:

> Vincent's canon is not a true "canon" nor an adequate criterion of church life. It does not take the eschatological status of the church seriously. It admits only of growth according to the inherent law of the church. It has no place for the powers of the age to come and for renewal by the Holy Spirit. Antiquity, universality and consent are not enough. The church is not only concerned with its own oneness, its universality and catholicity, but also with its holiness. And to be holy means to live in the strength of the new age.

Here the contrast is made clear between life, holiness, the new age, the age to come, renewal (all symbols of Christian spontaneity, inspired, at least in principle, by the Holy

---

[16] *Ecumenical Review*, 1958, 365–385.
[17] *The Renewal of the Church*, Philadelphia 1957, 65.

Spirit) and what is called "the inherent law of the church," the structure on which the body of the church builds itself as it grows. There is no denial of the need for structure. Visser 't Hooft says, in another passage, that the "unity which the churches must seek is not unity at any price, but on the contrary unity in deeper understanding of the specific nature and mission of the church," and that "the gift of renewal" is "for the upbuilding of the whole body in its unity."[18] This would imply a search for the structure inherent in her nature. Yet the stress remains on the "liberation of the church,"[19] freed by the Spirit from any ties to an abiding "ego-centricity and church-centeredness."[20]

The reactions of some Protestant circles to Roman Catholicism seem to arise from this "super-church complex," from this fear of structure even though the necessity for structure is also acknowledged. Some of the early reactions to the announcement by John XXIII of an ecumenical council may be understood in this sense. Dr. Eugene Carson Blake opined in April 1959 that the World Council had "more experience" in working for unity than the Roman Catholic Church. A statement from the Executive Committee of the World Council in February 1959 declared that "progress toward unity is made when churches meet together on the basis of mutual respect and with a full commitment on the part of each church to the

[18] Op. cit. 123.
[19] Op. cit. 97.
[20] Op. cit. 96.

truth of the Gospel, to charity and to a faithful interpretation of its deepest convictions."[21] These are sympathetic comments, though rather reserved and slightly defensive. Yet the notion that the Catholic Church has little experience in working for unity obviously betrays a preconceived conception of unity as life rather than as structure. For, starting from the opposite concept of unity as episcopal structure, one would have to conclude that the Catholic Church has more experience than others in promoting, protecting and explaining structural unity. Progress toward unity would also be made when churches meet together not only with "full commitment to the truth of Gospel," but also with full commitment to the search for a God-given stable structure.

It does also happen that when positive steps toward rapprochement are attempted on the part of the Catholic Church, some Protestant circles are gripped by fear, and life seems to be threatened by structure. The World Council, in which life has expressed its inventiveness, fears structure. Yet, as Alexander Schmemann has written, "although a Pan-Christian Council may be highly desirable, it cannot be, in terms of Orthodox ecclesiology, identified with an Ecumenical Council, the first being the 'expression' of the Ecumenical Movement, the second—the expression of the Church."[22] Here, the amorphous life seeking expression in

[21] As relayed by the Ecumenical Press Service, February 20, 1959.

[22] St. Vladimir Seminary Bulletin, Spring 1959, 40.

the ecumenical movement is clearly distinguished from the
structural life of the Church expressed in her hierarchy.
This suggests that the opposition between life and structure is largely artificial, and that the fear of a super-church
is, to a large extent, a psychological complex. Life and
structure, newness and tradition, can and must be ultimately reconciled in a concept of structural life, in a tradition understood, in the words of St. Vincent of Lerins, as
a *depositum juvenescens*, a youth-giving deposit.

The fear of a super-church, is, ultimately, the fear that
the structure of the church may be no other than the episcopal structure of the Catholic and the Orthodox churches.

Yet this fear has not been without good results. For at
least it prevents the World Council of stopping short at
any stage of its development and concluding that Christian
unity has been achieved in itself. The structure of the
church must, in the mind of Protestant ecumenism, be
manifested by the life of the churches, and particularly by
their common life in their growing unity. As a result, the
World Council cannot be a permanent feature of Christianity. It is only provisional, destined to disappear as soon as
the Spirit of life has revealed the ultimate structure of the
church in its renewed oneness. This was embodied in one
of the documents presented in 1954 to the Evanston Assembly: "Since the purpose of the Council is not to become
a federation, nor to become a World-Church by syntheti-
cally appropriating the diverse doctrine and polities of member churches, it must always look forward to its own de-
crease so that the manifestation of the oneness of the

church may increase."[23] The World Council is neither the Bridegroom nor the bride, but a friend preparing the meeting of the bride and the Bridegroom.

The search for religious unity implies a search for both the life and the structure of unity. The Catholic, the Orthodox and, to a lesser extent, the Anglican traditions believe that this structural life is given in the episcopal hierarchy. In some areas of the Protestant world, movements toward religious unity have precisely taken the form of attempts at restoring an episcopal structure without jeopardizing the specific features of Protestant freedom. Several such attempts are at the present time being negotiated in Asia and Africa, and the Church of South India presents the observer with a great advantage: the theory behind the reunion was outlined by one of its pioneers, Bishop Lesslie Newbigin. The South India scheme incorporated an episcopate borrowed from Anglicanism, and the former non-episcopal churches of that area now live within this ex-Anglican episcopal structure.

The starting point of Lesslie Newbigin comes from the basic Reformation doctrine of "justification by faith alone": man is *simul justus et peccator*.

To Luther and Calvin, Newbigin objects that they do not apply *simul justus et peccator* to the church as such. The church is not in this case the permanent result of an act of

[23] *Six Ecumenical Surveys*, New Delhi 1954, "Faith and Order," 43.

God which makes us just though we remain sinful. To this may be traced all the errors of Protestantism, especially the disappearance of the idea of the visible church, that is, its lack of concern for the structure of the church.

To Catholics, Newbigin objects that they deny the sinfulness of the church. Such a denial, he feels, subordinates the eschatological to the historical, life to structure. "Admittedly," he says, "no rational explanation can be given of the fact that the church, which is the Body of Christ, may sin. But only harm can come of denying a fact as plainly attested." Newbigin recognizes the need for "continuity in the transmission of authority." But this should not become absolute structure. For to absolutize the church's structure would be to forget "that the substance of the covenant is pure mercy: and that God retains His sovereign freedom to have mercy upon whom He wills and to call 'no People' His people when they that are called His people deny their calling by unbelief and sin."[24] In other words, the structure partakes too much of the sinful life of Christians to be an absolute.

The ecumenical movement is a dialogue between these two positions, between, as it were, life and structure. Yet Newbigin believes that it is in a deadlock so long as the dialogue does not become a trialogue. The rather chaotic "pentecostal" tradition should become a third partner. In pentecostals God has shown his good pleasure by blessing

[24] Lesslie Newbigin, The Household of God, New York 1954, 81.

them and, as Newbigin says, "those whom God has sealed we may not reject without dishonouring God." The Christian dilemma is three-cornered: life as faith, body as structure, and life as Spirit; Protestantism, Catholicism, Pentecostalism. "In recent discussions of the Catholic-Protestant issue and of the deadlock in which these discussions seem to have become immobilized, it is often suggested that the way forward may be found in a new understanding of the doctrine of the Holy Spirit."[25]

The church has to be all three: faith, body, spirit—at the same time. Yet, as seen by Newbigin, it is nowhere all three. Therefore the church is to be defined in terms not of what it is, but of what it is becoming. "The church is never to be finally defined in static terms, but only in terms of that to which it is going."[26] "We have . . . to conceive of the church in the perspective of a real *eschaton* for which we wait in faith and hope, still involved in this sinful age and yet living by the mercy of God. This acceptance of a real end means that the dimension of time is a reality within the life of the church, and that therefore we must ask of a church not only, What is it now? but, What is it becoming?"[27] This becoming is twofold. It is made of the church's tension toward the end of the world, the consummation of all things, the parousia, and her correlative tension toward the ends of the earth, trying to convert all

[25] Op. cit. 109.
[26] Op. cit. 25.
[27] Op. cit. 133–134.

nations while the day lasts. The "worldwide mission of the church . . . belongs to the very core of its existence as a corporate body."[28]

The church is defined by its becoming, and nobody knows for sure what it is becoming. Then we cannot define the structural life of the church before it unfolds itself. We can only wait for God's practical guidance. In the present ecumenical debate, "the solution—and this is of vital importance—will be a solution in which theory and practice are inseparably related, not one which can satisfactorily be stated in terms of theory alone."[29] No one can invent a blueprint for a united church. We have to trust ourselves to God in a "uniting church."

In this theology, the quest for the structure of unity presents the undeniable advantage of being truly related to life. It is a quest for structural life or, equivalently, for living structure. The dilemma of much Protestant ecumenism, caught between life and structure, seeing yet fearing the necessity of structure, has been overcome. Structure appears in terms of life and life is essentially the manifestation of structure.

To the quest for structure and for structural life to which the ecumenical movement amounts, Catholic theology would say that the Christian life itself, through its sacramental framework, is structured, and that the church's

[28] Op. cit. 143.
[29] Op. cit. 25.

episcopal and sacramental structure is, by the grace of God, life-giving. Thus the dilemma between structure and life is, ultimately, a false dilemma. The pentecostal tradition, which includes elements of "enthusiasm" or false mysticism, cannot help much to rise above the dilemma. What we need is to understand both Christian life and Christian hierarchy in their biblical and patristic meaning. The Catholic and the Orthodox traditions embody this meaning. The quest for Christian unity should therefore ultimately reach fruition in an integration of Protestantism within the Catholic-Orthodox church-pattern.

Yet one should beware the Catholic temptation: to insist on structure at the expense of life. Orthodox theology has not felt this temptation so much as Catholic theology, largely because of its less legalistic approach to the structure of the church. The church as *sobor*, Catholicity as *sobornost*, never oppose spontaneity, for they include the spontaneity of the Holy Spirit. The way for Catholics to overcome their frequently legalistic view of the movement toward religious unity is to meditate on the patristic ecclesiology as it is still visible in Orthodoxy. This ecclesiology lies at the root of the development which is Roman Catholicism: and developments are best understood in their source.

Is it by a mere accident of history, or by one of those unforeseen interventions of the Spirit that, under the impact of Pope John XXIII, Catholicism today is thinking of itself in terms of a council? *Sobor* means council. A council is a meeting of the hierarchy with a view to formulating the doctrine, and channeling the life, of the Church. It is a manifestation of life as interpreted by structure. One should not be over optimistic to the concrete possibilities of re-union in the near future. Yet the Catholic concern for structural life is today closer than at any time before to the search for structure within the spontaneity of life which is manifested in the ecumenical movement. Thus we may hope that the quest for structure in the modern movement for religious unity will discover that the sacramental order is itself the life of the Spirit in the faithful and the structure given by God to his people.

10 THE MISSIONARY CHURCH

The popular conception of missions is simple: a missionary goes to a foreign country which is supposed to need more enlightenment than his own does. He preaches the Gospel and brings pagans into the Church. In so doing he helps them save their souls, or at least he helps them reach heaven in the most appropriate way, the conscious following of our Savior, Jesus Christ. On this basis and for this purpose many missionary vocations have been born. Men have heard the call to follow the example of our father Abraham, to "leave their country and the house of their father" and to go like the apostles where the Spirit would lead, preaching the Gospel to all nations.

A mission in this sense is an outpost of the Church in a non-Christian environment. It is an embassy of the Church to the "world." The Church, the mystical body of Christ, the organism of salvation, reaches out to the world in order to transform it. She gives it a chance to hear the Lord's voice and heed it, to become something other than the "world" for which Jesus did not pray, to be made into the Church.

Not everything is false in this conception of missions. Preaching the Gospel to all nations requires a specialized

body of "missionaries." These have to make themselves
"all things to all men" in areas that are remote, in terms of
geography, from the great Catholic centers: primitive, in
terms of civilization, by comparison with the western world
with which, for better or for worse, the Church has been
identified; and pagan, where non-Christian religions predominate.

Yet it would be wrong to conceive missions only in terms
of the salvation of individuals. The Church is not primarily
concerned with the salvation of souls. She is not directly
responsible for the reception or rejection of the Gospel by
those to whom she brings it. The apostles were not told to
worry if people would not listen to them; they were instructed simply to go to another place. It does not belong
to the Church to separate the sheep from the goats. God
will know his own even where the Church has not been
listened to, just as he will know his enemies, if there are
some, within the gate, the false brethren inside of the
Church.

It would also be wrong to conceive the mission as an activity in which not all Christians need to take part. It is not
enough to support the missions by sending them occasional
offerings. The missions are not only a specialized activity
far away from us, a sort of pioneering far from the base-
camps.

The following principle is essential to an understanding
of a theology of the missions: it is not the missioner who is
missionary, it is the Church. The Church is missionary
because her very nature consists in being, in this world,

a foretaste of the world to come. The center of her life, which is the holy Eucharist, is a memorial of the past in view of the future, "announcing the Lord's death until he come." But when the past and the future coincide with the present moment, we have more than past, present or future: we have an eternal present, eternity, a participation, here on earth, in the very life of God. This relates immediately to the nature of missions. For preaching the good news of salvation makes the word of God echo in time; it brings the eternal into the texture of history. The center of all presentation of the Gospel is precisely the sacramental act by which the Church communes with her Lord. This liturgical action constitutes God's embassy to the world; it is the sacrifice in which heaven receives the first-fruits of redemption in the form of the body and blood of Christ; and it is the offering in which heaven receives the first-born from among the dead, the resurrected Christ. If the Church's mission consists in preaching the Gospel, the liturgy forms the core of this preaching. And no other preaching is legitimate unless it is related to this. Every activity—be it teaching or doing—which is an extension of this is missionary. An activity which is not an extension of this cannot be missionary.

In other words, the mission is not a specialized apostolate. It is not the property of missionary congregations or societies; nor is it the sum total of all missionary groups. It is not restricted to what is deliberately done for the propagation of the faith. The mission is the whole Church. The liturgical life of the whole Church has a missionary structure. She holds herself in readiness to announce the coming of the Lord. Her existence is a proclamation that the Lord is coming, that this world will pass and make way for the world of which it is but a shadow and a foretaste.

What is true of the Eucharist applies also to the other aspects of the Church, even to her most institutional ones. Our modern civilization, with its awareness of sociology and its organizational efficiency, sees the Church's hierarchy as a convenient device comparable to the organization of secular corporations. In the older view, which dominated the thought of the Church fathers, the hierarchy was an image, here on earth, of the plurality in unity which constitutes the inner life of God. The interrelationships of the Father, the Son and the Spirit have an analogy in the Church in the interrelationships of the bishop, the priests and the laity, all distinct in their function, yet one in the "new nature" received in baptism. The Church's visible hierarchy is a sign of the invisible hierarchy of God. It has the prophetic meaning of elevating human relationships to the level of the divine and, conversely, of presenting man with a divine pattern for interpersonal relations. Once more, the Church is in a state of missionary preparedness: she describes the life of God in human language; she foretells the ultimate aim of human relations by making their divine model present to us. This is her mission.

As seen in more pragmatic terms, the Church's mission is twofold. The Church is missionary in relation to the world, because she first of all is missionary in relation to herself. She can preach the Gospel to pagans only because she preaches it to her members. She can preach to non-Christians because she keeps preaching to Christians, reminding them of the good news that they have heard, placing before them an image of God's own life, introducing and re-introducing them constantly to the heavenly life through their liturgical experience, making them look forward, in longing expectation, to the return of their Lord. The very meaning of the period of Advent is just this: the Church is missionary to her members; we are expecting the coming of Christ; we are preparing ourselves to receive him, for he is on the way.

From this essential missionary meaning of the Church we can easily pass to the specialized activity of those whom we call missionaries. Through them the Church preaches to the pagan world what she keeps repeating to herself. They prepare the ground for this self-mission or this mission-to-self which is the Church. Their first problem is not to save souls. It is to build the Church as a prophetic agent in a pagan environment. Their purpose is not individualistic. It does not aim at saving or converting individuals. It is corporate and organic: it aims at rooting the Church, with her hierarchical organization and her liturgical life, in a new human gound. It anticipates what the Church will be when she is fully established in this new territory, this new civilization or this new culture. Only then will the mission be fulfilled, when the Church testifies to her Lord by "announcing his death until he come" in the language of a new people.

What this entails as regards the pedagogy of preaching

need not be detailed out here. Yet some missiological implications should be listed: missionaries should divest themselves of their native culture in order to embrace the culture
of those among whom they live; they should respect the
forms of Christian life that nonwestern countries may discover; they ought to cherish the insights into Catholic
doctrine that western thinking has not acquired and that
may be the privilege of other races and cultures; they ought
to look for the enrichment that will come to the Church
from African and Asian spiritual experiences and intellectual achievements. All this should be investigated for an
adequate missiology.

American Catholicism has entered the field of foreign
missions. Its missionaries are at work in many lands, in
Africa, Asia, Oceania, Central and South America and in
many sections that are not canonically classified as foreign
missions. This contribution of American priests and sisters
to the Church's task of preaching the Gospel to all nations
deserves to be acknowledged. American Catholics are also
present in foreign missions as lay apostles. Among lay missionary groups Americans are beginning to take an important place.

All this is good. It belongs to the coming of age of
American Catholicism. Yet this will not detain us for the
present. Foreign missions are one overflow of the missionary urge. They are neither the first nor the most important
manifestation of the missionary spirit. Should the Church,
owing to extraordinary circumstances, close her foreign missions, she would still remain missionary to herself. She

would still be the herald of God's kingdom. And her mission primarily consists in this. The problem of the missionary role of the American Church is not to find out how much money we can give to the propagation of the faith, how many boys and girls we can send to missionary congregations, how many native seminarians we can support, how many parcels we can send to the needy in other parts of the world. The problem is both much more simple and much more difficult. How do American Catholics fulfill their role of anticipating the kingdom of heaven here on earth, of witnessing to the Lord's presence, of transforming the world to a better image of its Maker? Does the Church in the United States develop a missionary consciousness? Do her children learn that *they* cannot save anybody's soul, even their own, but that their only duty is to witness to the Lord's coming? What "eschatological" dimension is there in American Catholicism?

It is very simple to answer these questions. For it necessitates no schemes, no plan, no blueprint, no schedule. It only requires the knowledge of what Christianity is: the presence of the Savior in the community of those whom he saves. And yet it is immensely difficult. For it implies a self-criticism which human nature is reluctant to make. It is always difficult to recognize that we may be good Catholics in a wrong way. All Catholics need to proceed to this self-criticism, unless they claim that they have reached perfection. But if they make this claim, they have to support it; then they will run into trouble.

The missionary role of the American Church may be

assessed from the point of view of her responsibility at home. What the Church does in relation to her environment depends on her willingness to deepen her missionary dimension. The Church is not missionary by trying to convert all Americans, but rather by witnessing to her faith in the peculiar circumstances of the American background. The pluralism of American society presents the Church with an extraordinary opportunity to show that she is open, by her very nature, to all cultures and mentalities. The Church in the world at large must be Catholic rather than Latin, Italian, Spanish or German; likewise, the Church in America must be Catholic rather than Irish, Polish or Italian. She must not be the Church of a national or cultural minority. She must not let herself be identified with the special interests of football teams or pressure groups. American Catholics in the past have had reasons to be very much concerned about being American to the Americans. In a comedy which purports to give a picture of American life, "La Mouche Bleue," the playwright Marcel Aymé has felt that he could not present American society without a Catholic priest. The Protestant minister in this play answers all difficult questions by singing a hymn. The Catholic priest finds the solution of all problems in proclaiming the blessings of God on capitalism. Clearly this is a satire. But the caricature has a point: do we impress our contemporaries (non-Catholics around us, or Catholics abroad) with the catholicity of our thinking? The gum-chewing, "nice guy" priest of the Hollywood movies may be a good sample of what an average American is assumed to look like, but he is not a witness to the dimension of catholicity. Yet without the full dimension of catholicity the Church is not truly a missionary Church; she cannot witness to the Eternal who has come in the incarnation, who is coming in the liturgy and who will come again to judge the living and the dead.

It seems that the missionary readiness of the American Church will be tested on three main grounds: Catholic-Protestant relations; social justice; the intellectual apostolate. I shall deal more at length with the first.

Two conceptions of Catholic-Protestant relations should be eliminated. Both are found among Catholics and Protestants. Yet neither is adequate.

The first attitude to be discarded sees Catholicism and Protestantism as competing pressure groups. In American democracy as it has evolved, lobbying plays an important role in the process of making and testing laws. Business groups, unions, minority groups, zealous organizations for the defense of public morality have recourse to more or less open pressuring. At best they pressure public opinions, which in turn will pressure the legislators. Political life is made of the competition of innumerable pressure groups. Religious societies may also conceive of their role on the pattern of pressure groups.

This raises the following question: do Catholics behave as though the Church were a pressure group? Do they, by their behavior, make her forcibly into one? Concerning the American Church as a whole, the answer must be negative. Yet it is clear that many Catholics do behave in this manner. For them the Church competes with other denominations for the allegiance of the American people. Thus they make her a rival among rivals, a sect among sects. But a church which is a pressure group intent on neutralizing the influence of Protestant denominations is not the Great Church recognizable by the fact that she may have imitators, but she can have no rivals; she may have enemies, but she is enemy to no one; others may be jealous of her, but she is jealous of no one; she may be attacked, but she need not defend herself. Her true defense does not lie in polemics or in apologetics, but in witnessing to a glory which is not hers, but Christ's, to a truth which is not her own, but which owns her, to a faith which she does not grasp like a possession, but which grasps her. The Church in her missionary status has nothing to defend, nothing to protect, nothing to shelter; she has everything to offer and everything to give. In the death of her Lord she knows his resurrection. And in being persecuted for justice's sake, if need be, she is certain of her victory over the gates of hell. Her policy in regard to other religious groups is one of nonviolence. It can be nothing less or more. Less then nonviolence would be acquiescence. But the Church cannot consent to religious positions or doctrines that are not her own. Her universality means that she is the fullness of all that God does on this earth. There is nothing outside of her because she extends to God's entire action in our world. To agree to doctrines or conceptions that are outside her full tradition would jeopardize her universality. This she cannot do, for she stands or falls with her fidelity to herself. Something more than nonviolence under the pressure of would-be rivals would violate her integrity. It would itself be, even in a mild form, a recourse to violence. This would impede her preaching the Gospel of the One who is "meek and humble of heart," of the Lamb of God who was drawn to the slaughter house and did not utter one cry. There undoubtedly exist pressure groups organized by Catholics and waving the banner of Catholicism. They should seriously examine if they do not constitute a threat which is more dangerous to the Church than it is to her so-called adversaries.

In the second place, Catholic-Protestant relations must not be conceived on a purely individual plane. Because we all meet Protestants in various capacities, we have to work out a system of coexistence. Most of us systematically ignore people's religion in order to get along on the neutral field of business or social intercourse. Others, who probably feel more or less insecure in their Catholicism, are on the defensive, being argumentative in and out of season; to others they seem bigoted and they convey the mistaken impression that a good Catholic should always be on the look out for arguments about the faith; they think it their duty constantly to defend the Church, as though she needs them for survival. Others still, without being aggressive or unduly apologetic, lie in wait for an opening into which they can wedge a suggestion of conversion; the attitude that they adopt is proselytism; if they have a Protestant in their family, they make his life miserable until conversion seems the only escape.

Admittedly, this sounds exaggerated. Yet any Catholic can identify persons whom these descriptions fit. These persons have made the mistake of viewing the relations of Protestants and Catholics on a strictly individualistic level. But the Church is not an individual. Her unity is the oneness of a collectivity, kept together by the act through which the Lord gives himself to her. This brings us back to the holy Eucharist. The Church's unity is not aggressive like a military alliance or a power-political coalition. It is a liturgical unity, made of her ever-renewed experience of encountering the Lord in the community meal of the holy Eucharist. At this level there are not two or three ways of looking at Protestantism; there is no choice between several types of behavior toward non-Catholic Christians. Only the attitude of humble service is satisfactory. Anything less than this is not worthy of the Church. The Church exists to serve men, whether these are inside or outside her visible limits. The only way in which we can show the Church in her missionary dimension in relation to Protestant Christians consists in a collective approach through service. To competition and rivalry we ought to substitute fraternity. This is, in a word, the ecumenical attitude.

The question may be asked: how would this fulfill the missionary calling of the Church? After all, as is sometimes said, "we have the truth and we proclaim it boldly to the world; we do want conversions, for such is the mission of the Church." If we do want conversions we can only be aggressive in our proclamation of the truth.

This conclusion is a fallacy. The Church's mission is not directly to save souls or to make converts. This individualistic approach is just as false as regards Protestant Christians as it is in the matter of foreign missions. The Church is missionary when she announces the kingdom of God through the essential acts of her existence, through the "eschatological" dimension of her life and doctrine. She is missionary to pagans when she builds in their midst the dimension of Catholicity which binds together heaven and earth. Likewise, she is missionary to Protestants when she contributes to a restoration, in Protestantism as a whole, of the catholic dimension which Protestantism has lost. There can only be one catholicity; and therefore the ultimate outcome of this restoration must be the reunion of Christendom. But the Church's aim is not the negative purpose of destroying Protestantism through a war of attrition; it is the positive aim of building up Protestant Christianity to the fullness of Catholicity which is the Church.

The American Church lives in a predominately Protestant culture. This should be the best possible position to start an ecumenical program. True, the nature of American Protestantism makes this more difficult than it would be in countries where Protestantism is homogeneous. The challenge, however, is worth a special effort. Here lies the main missionary task of the American Church. There should be in America, Catholic ecumenical centers, as there are several in Europe, which would provide the Catholic press with adequate information concerning Protestantism and the ecumenical movement. Catholic papers often are misinformed and misinterpret the news relating to these matters; they then unwittingly misinform their reading public. Such institutes could also establish spiritual and intellectual contacts with Protestants, encourage theological meetings and support sound literature in this field. This will have to be done if we want the Church in America to be true to her missionary calling.

An ecumenical attitude cannot be created out of nothing. It must be based on a generous understanding of Catholicity. And this must naturally flourish in a broad humanism. Catholicism is interested in man as man. Man himself, in his full humanity, has attracted the redemptive love of God after having been made out of God's creative love. The message of eternal love which constitutes the Church as missionary is also addressed to man as such, independently of cultural differentiations and even in total disregard of his religion or irreligion. Whatever god a man adores, this man is called to know the true God. The man that God wants to espouse for eternity is not the European, the American, the Asian, the westerner or the easterner; he is every man in his singularity and his universality.

In other words, every movement that is at the service of man, every humanism, every vision of a better mankind deserves respect. It is a psychological impossibility to respect the true religion without a minimum esteem for false religions; for one cannot take the true religion seriously unless one has taken seriously every religious aspiration of man. The true religion is not built in opposition to false religions. The true God is not a rival of false gods; he is their redeemer.

How does this apply to the missionary role of the American Church? Catholicism implies a generous humanism. And Catholics should place themselves at the service of every effort to achieve the ideal mankind in modern society. This requires an opening of the mind and the heart to the intellectual movements of the day, be they secularist or agnostic. It also requires an awareness of social justice, for which so many sections of society have been fighting, here and elsewhere. The missionary role of the American Church is not over when we have defined our social doctrine. It will be over only when social justice has been guaranteed to all. Likewise, our intellectual responsibility does not lie in reading St. Thomas in second-rate translations; it lies in finding a common ground with the intellectual movements today.

This may be far from the strictly "churchly" activity of teaching and baptizing. But let us never forget that we lie if we preach truth without also preaching love. And love can never remain a platonic declaration of abstract philanthropy. It is existential and seeks expression in concrete actions. Love is incarnate. It has nothing in common with a discarnate teaching.

I have tried to outline a synthetic approach to the missionary role of the American Church. This would have only slightly differed had I outlined the missionary role of the Church in other countries. The principles are the same everywhere, although circumstances call for emphasis on one or another aspect of the Church's mission. In America today circumstances demand a new look at the responsibility of Catholics in ecumenical matters, in intellectual fields and social justice.

Yet a condition is to be fulfilled before we can develop this approach on a large scale. The mission is primarily a mission of the Church to herself. It is the announcement of the Gospel as the anticipation of the kingdom of God; it is the commemoration of the Lord's death until he comes. The Church constantly calls herself to be faithful to her Lord. Depth calls to depth. The Church enters deeper and deeper into the implications of her faith. Somewhere along these implications she discovers her ecumenical, intellectual and social obligations and opportunities. But how can we reach so far unless we take part as we should in the Church's communion with Christ, in the liturgical mystery which lies at the heart of her mission? That is to say, there is no missionary movement without a spiritual revival. There is no social justice without the justice of the sacramental order. There is no Catholic intellectualism without the breadth of "the common life in the body of Christ." At the basis of every missionary endeavor lies the mystery of the liturgy. Nothing shall be achieved in missionary fields unless we first renovate ourselves spiritually.